INTERNATIONAL TRADE POLICY

International Trade Policy: A Developing-Country Perspective

Dilip K. Das
Professor and Area Chairman
Indian Institute of Management, Lucknow

MACMILLAN

First published 1990

Published by
THE MACMILLAN PRESS LTD
Houndmills, Basingstoke, Hampshire RG21 2XS
and London
Companies and representatives
throughout the world

Printed in Hong Kong

British Library Cataloguing in Publication Data
Das, Dilip K., *1945–*
International trade policy: a developing country
perspective.
1. Developing countries. Foreign trade. Policies of
government
I. Title
382'.3'091724

ISBN 0–333–51152–2

For
Tanushree
and
Siddharth

Contents

Acronyms and Initials

GATT	General Agreement on Tariffs and Trade
GSP	Generalised System of Preferences
ICOR	Incremental Capital Output Ratio
IMF	International Monetary Fund
ITO	International Trade Organisation
LDC	Less Developed Country
MFA	Multifibre Arrangement
MFN	Most-Favoured-Nation
MTN	Multilateral Trade Negotiations
NBER	National Bureau of Economic Research
NIC	Newly Industrialising Country
NTB	Non-Tariff Barrier
OMA	Orderly Marketing Arrangement
QRs	Quantitative Restrictions
REER	Real Effective Exchange Rate
TNC	Trade Negotiation Committee
VER	Voluntary Export Restraints

List of Tables

Preface

The primal objective of this book is to bring theory and knowledge of the economics of international trade to bear on the policy decisions in the developing countries. I try to bring together the academic research and the real life trade issues, without 'blue yondering'. The unification of analysis and policy-making was, according to Plato, the function of the philosopher king. In our age it has been taken over by the trade economists and the mandarins in the national and supranational systems. The binding element in this book is neither the depth nor the intensity of research, but an eagerness to relate policy-making to positive trade economics so that optimal decisions are arrived at, and, in the process, the developing countries are able to solve their complex growth problems as well as integrate into the international economy.

There is little doubt that the majority of developing economies fall short of their productive potential. Yet a handful of them have done a superlative job. One of the factors which helped this group of developing countries was that they followed a different kind of trade policy package from the rest. It is now generally realised that the level of economic efficiency achieved in an economy is determined by the degree of openness, and the trade policy package adopted by the developing country in question. The trade policies also have a decisive and measurable impact on employment and output.

That economic liberalisation and adoption of a neutral policy package can lead to a dramatic turn around in a developing economy is well known. Chile and Taiwan are two excellent recent illustrations of this fact. Yet soft thinking regarding trade policy is ubiquitous. Most developing countries still have illiberal and controlled policy regimes. Serious policy errors leading to welfare contracting outcomes are commonplace. The repercussions of the policy actions are not limited to the domestic economy; they transcend national boundaries. Therefore, the proposed policy package also needs to be judged in the international context. The developing country perspective, it seems, includes a less complete appreciation of the value and fragility of a coherent international trading system. At times it is also based on the mercantilistic fallacies.

The trade policies have been the victim of more than their share of bad economics in a large number of developing countries. In this book I take my inspiration from the standard neo-classical economic theory in order to counter misleading ideas, false concepts and invalid theoretical premises. I agree with the neo-classical economists in their emphasis on the appropriateness of domestic policies and their welfare implications. I go one step ahead and recommend an economic and organisational structure which would enable a developing country to benefit from its potential comparative advantage.

Since the early 1970s the international economy has been buffeted by many exogenous shocks. The shifting pattern of comparative advantage and the sharpened competitiveness of a sub-set of developing countries have added to the complexities, and the industrialised countries have been sorely tempted to adopt protectionist policies. In fact, many of them have already succumbed to accepting protectionism as a way of contemporary economic life. Several industrialised countries, in particular the large traders, have taken measures to control developing countries' access to their markets. These policy actions have made the present international trading regime neurotically protectionist, which undermines productivity and growth in the world economy.

On one hand, the developed countries have encouraged the developing countries to become the Contracting Parties of the GATT and allowed them several concessions under Article XVIII and Part IV of the GATT Charter. They have accepted the formal derogation from the principle of non-discrimination, the foundation-stone of the GATT, to permit the establishment of the Generalised System of Preferences. On the other hand, developing countries, in particular the newly industrialising ones, face a progressively increasing number of discriminatory protectionist measures against their exports. What is more baneful, the export-restricting arrangements are negotiated outside the framework of the GATT.

The industrialised and the developing countries have reached an impasse in their trade relations. At the time of writing this prefatory note, the multilateral negotiations under the Uruguay Round were, at best, making a plodding progress. The mid-term review conference of the trade ministers, held in Montreal in December 1988, brought to the fore several major contentious issues between the negotiating country groups. The positions held by them were wide apart, with each group taking a self-righteously intransigent stand.

Inasmuch as the international trade strategies need to be judged in national and international contexts, this book deals with the domestic and international aspect of trade policy from the perspective of the developing countries. Its scope also encompasses the issue generated out of an interaction between the industrialised and developing countries in the international trade arena. It is hoped that it will benefit both students and researchers in the field of international trade as well as bureaucrats and functionaries in national and international organisations related to trade.

DILIP K. DAS

Free trade, like honesty, is still the best policy.

— *An apostle of the gospel of free trade.*

1 The Contemporary Trade Scenario

1 THE ISSUE

The formulation of an effective macro-economic policy package is one of the key ingredients for self-sustained long-term growth, and international trade strategies are an integral part of it. Sagacious trade policies help increase economic welfare by achieving a better allocation of resources; therefore they have been a focal point of analysis for international trade economists and policy planners for the last three and a half decades. On numerous occasions trade economists have noted with concern that the policies adopted by planners in many less developed countries (LDCs) have been widely at variance with those emanating from the models of optimal resource allocation. Some less developed countries, after pursuing a certain trade policy package, affected a significant reversal in the strategy, and were pleasantly surprised by the dramatic favourable results.

A healthy trade expansion is, indeed, not a sufficient condition for rapid and sustained growth, because in the ultimate analysis economic growth depends primarily upon the national policy variables. However, there are few cases in which rapid growth has been achieved without trade expansion. International trade *inter alia* generates the benefits of specialisation and the economies of scale.

There are not only static gains to be derived from trade expansion, like more efficient use of a country's existing resources, but also there are dynamic gains through the new investment, increased knowledge and improvement in skills. In short, international trade provides for the extension of domestic opportunities available for converting resources into goods and services required for investment and consumption. With expanding trade comes greater foreign exchange earnings and expansion in capital stock, leading to higher incomes, which, in turn, results in extra capital formation. In addition, trade expansion in an LDC enhances the capacity to import, including imports of capital goods and technology, which again stimulates the export sector and a 'virtuous circle' is established leading the developing economy on a self-sustained growth path. Increased trade influences the structure and vitality of the entire economy.

Another dynamic gain is that international competition enormously improves domestic economic efficiency. Trade expansion also increases an LDC's ability to borrow and service debt. It stimulates entrepreneurship by expanding markets and by providing exposure to new products, and new ideas and standards of excellence. We shall delve into the trade-growth link in the next chapter.

For these reasons, LDCs have an important stake in international trade and the international trading environment. Both the liberalisation of their own economies on the one hand, and the maintenance of an open international trading system on the other, are crucially important for their growth prospects. An open, liberal, multilateral trading system provides them with access to markets, which is essential if LDCs are to achieve maximum gains from well-designed trade and domestic macro-economic policies. A smooth and unobtrusive trading environment is seen as a necessary, but not sufficient, condition for growth in the developing and industrialised economies. Should the international trading system erode and trade opportunities be stifled by the rising tide of protectionism, the prospects for rapid growth in developing and industrialised economies would grow dim. To be sure, the industrialised countries also have an important stake in the international trading system, but it is the new entrants to the trade scene that stand to lose the most from a restrained international trading regime.

2 THE THEORETICAL RATIONALE OF THE POLICY

Over the last three and a half decades a great deal has been learned and unlearned about the significance of trade theory and policy in the macro-economic policy package of the LDCs. Initially the majority of economists were sceptical about the relevance of the traditional neo-classical approach and policy prescriptions. They contended that the maxim that a liberal

international trade and payments regime yielded mutual benefits to all the partners did not hold good for LDCs. Uncertainty
was rife about the ability of LDCs to expand their exports. The
admonitions of Ragner Nurkse, Gunnar Myrdal and Raul
Prebisch about elasticity pessimism and a secular decline in the
terms of trade of the LDCs were fresh in the air, and had
become part of the conventional wisdom. Also in doubt was the
capacity of LDCs for industrial growth, without high walls of
protection. The first wave of export pessimism[1] was based on
an assessment of the natural market forces. It was believed that
the markets were not deep enough to absorb the expanding
exports – mostly of primary commodities – of the developing
countries. What exacerbated the pessimism was the worry that
synthetics were replacing natural products and that technological progress was simultaneously reducing inputs per unit of
output. These arguments were not far fetched, yet the scepticism subsequently proved to be ill-founded because of three
phenomena: first, the empirical evidence failed to support the
elasticity pessimism hypothesis. Second, the protectionist strategy was found to be full of lacuna and weak, and some of those
who supported it later became its unequivocal critics. Third, the
experiences of those LDCs that had adopted a neutral strategy,
without a bias against exports, or one that was outward-
looking, were far more rewarding than those that did not.

The trade policy issues and their practical application are
inherently complex. They embrace policies related to the overall
macro balance of the economy as well as setting of incentives in
a vast range of industries. They also entail exchange rate
policies. Therefore, a proper theoretical perspective of these
issues is highly significant. Sound theoretical knowledge can
lead to sagacious policy decisions, yet it is difficult to gauge the
quantitative significance of these decisions for the economy.
How can one say with certitude which policy package has been
more or less efficient and effective? The difficulty arises because
myriad other changes are taking place in the environment where
this policy is being implemented. This makes it difficult for the
analyst to come to 'iron-clad conclusions' about the strategy
based on one country or one period of experience. The practical
experiences of several successful and not-so-successful LDCs
have been revealing in this regard. They could, through cumulative evidence, build up a firmer basis for judgement. Several
major studies adopted this approach.

Notable progress and refinements have been made in the theoretical analysis, including the present tendency to make a distinction between domestic distortions and foreign trade distortions. An important analytical development was the development of the concept of effective protection – courtesy Max Cordon. It demonstrated that the same nominal tariff rate might imply very different rates of protection to value added for producers of different items. This concept brings out the unfeasibility of a 'rational' protectionist structure, because a uniform nominal tariff is not a uniformly effective tariff.

It is commonly observed that trade policy in most LDCs treats different traded goods differently. Usually activities that save foreign exchange receive very different sets of incentives from those that earn foreign exchange. Also, goods that save foreign exchange are given different incentives according to the sector to which they belong. There are four major sectors from this perspective, namely, agricultural and manufacturing sectors producing goods for exports, plus agricultural and manufacturing sectors producing goods that substitute for imports. In LDCs trade policy generally discriminates in favour of one of them, namely, manufacturing for import substitution.[2] The discrimination is done through the use of import prohibitions and high import tariffs on manufactured goods. It is seldom seen that an import tariff of 50 per cent on manufactured goods allows the import-competing manufacturing sector to use 50 per cent more real resources per dollar (assuming the exporting country is the United States) saved, than (1) what export activities are allowed per dollar generated or (2) what import-competing agriculture is allowed per dollar saved. The trade strategy is considered an important influence on the effectiveness with which other factors of production are employed.

An increasing number of LDCs are trying to achieve a domestic trade and external payments policy regime that would actively encourage economic growth, and hoping for a stimulating international trading environment. This book is addressed to clearing the cobwebs of confusion and misgivings that are so ubiquitous in the realm of trade policy, and underscoring the economic relationships that are important for formulating an efficient and effective policy structure. It proposes to focus on both facets of trade policy, the domestic and the international, from the perspective of the developing countries.

There is an apt lesson for the LDCs to extract out of the international trade dynamics of the last two decades. The conclusion that the dynamic exporters are those that are also the dynamic importers, cannot escape them. The evidence of this can be seen in Table 1.1 below, which ranks economies by the average annual rate of growth in the dollar value of their merchandise exports between 1970 and 1987, that is, by their long-term growth rates. Seventeen of the 30 economies in this table reporting above average export growth between 1970 and 1987 also report above average import growth over this period. For the period 1982 to 1987, the evidence is even more striking, with 28 out of 32 economies showing rapid export *and* import growth. The trade dynamics cut across any single classification in terms of size, stage of development or geography. Among the economies showing well above average long-term growth rates, there are industrial economies as well as the developing ones, and there are economies from Africa, Asia, Latin America as well as those from Western Europe and North America.

Table 1.1 GROWTH OF MERCHANDISE TRADE VALUE FOR SELECTED ECONOMIES, 1970–87
(Average annual percentage change)

Exports (f.o.b.)			Imports (c.i.f.)	
1970–87	1982–87		1970–87	1982–87
26.8	16.7	Korea, Rep. of	19.5	11.1
23.5	19.2	Taiwan	20.1	12.8
19.0	18.2	Hong Kong[a]	18.0	15.5
18.7	6.7	Singapore[a]	16.4	2.9
18.3	12.1	Turkey	16.8	8.5
18.2	12.6	China	18.9	18.1
17.9	10.9	Thailand	14.5	8.7
17.2	−5.8	Indonesia	16.5	−4.4
17.2	−0.3	Mexico	10.2	−3.4
16.9	14.7	Ireland	13.3	7.0
16.9	10.6	Spain	14.7	9.2
15.7	10.8	Japan	13.0	2.8
15.6	1.5	Tunisia	14.5	−2.3
15.0	9.8	Israel	12.0	7.0
14.9	−1.0	Ecuador	12.6	0.6

14.9	8.3	Malaysia	13.8	0.5
14.8	11.7	Pakistan	13.0	1.3
14.3	17.1	Portugal	13.5	7.0
14.2	5.4	Brazil	10.9	-4.7
14.2	11.7	Austria	14.0	10.9
14.0	14.9	Iceland	14.6	10.9
14.0	6.7	Greece	11.3	3.7
13.8	−22.9	Saudi Arabia	22.0	−12.5
13.8	11.8	Switzerland	13.0	12.0
13.7	4.3	Norway	11.2	7.9
13.7	9.6	Italy	13.3	7.5
13.6	8.9	Finland	12.6	8.1
13.5	10.8	Germany, Fed. Rep.	12.7	8.0
13.4	4.4	USSR[b]	13.0	4.3
13.2	8.9	France	13.2	6.5
13.0	6.9	Netherlands	12.0	7.4
12.9	6.9	Bulgaria[b]	13.8	7.1
12.7	10.7	Denmark	10.9	8.8
12.4	6.7	Hungary	12.0	7.5
12.4	9.9	Belgium-Luxembourg	12.4	7.4
11.9	2.1	Yugoslavia	9.1	−1.3
11.9	6.2	United Kingdom	12.2	9.1
11.7	10.7	Sweden	10.9	8.1
11.5	8.7	Colombia	10.1	−4.5
11.1	7.8	Czechoslovakia[b]	11.4	8.3
11.1	4.6	German Dem. Rep.[b]	10.6	4.2
11.0	5.3	New Zealand	10.9	4.7
10.9	3.1	United States	14.5	10.7
10.9	6.4	Canada	11.6	9.6
10.7	−10.5	Nigeria	9.6	−23.2
10.7	3.9	India	12.9	2.3
10.6	3.8	Australia	10.9	1.9
10.6	5.5	Morocco	11.1	−1.0
10.4	2.5	Philippines	10.6	−3.7
10.1	3.1	Uruguay	9.9	0.6
13.0	6.1	World	13.2	6.2

[a]Includes substantial re-exports and imports for re-exports.
[b]Imports, f.o.b.
Source: General Agreement on Tariffs and Trade, *International Trade 1987/88*. Geneva, 1988, Table 13, p. 36.

3 TRENDS IN LDC TRADE

During the 1970s the LDCs increased their share in the value of world trade; it rose from 19.0 per cent in 1973 to 28.7 per cent in 1980. Three quarters of this increase was due to the greater relative importance of trade in fuels. Of late, the share of LDCs in world trade has declined; it stood at 27.0 per cent in 1985 and 25.2 per cent in 1986. According to the *Direction of Trade Statistics* yearbook (1987), LDC exports declined considerably during 1986, by 5.6 per cent. At the same time imports increased moderately, up by 2.7 per cent. After registering surpluses in 1984 and 1985, the aggregate trade balance of LDCs shifted to a deficit of $35 billion in 1986.[3] This was the result of a deterioration in their terms of trade, caused by a sharp drop in oil prices and weakness in the prices of other primary commodities. The combined UN index of the prices of major primary commodities of interest to LDCs, which started rising in the early 1970s, peaked in 1980, and began falling at an average annual rate of nearly 5 per cent.

The majority of LDCs still depend on primary commodities – basic foods and industrial raw materials – for their foreign exchange earnings. The commodity price depression noted in the preceding paragraph reflects several fundamental changes in the use of raw materials in the industrialised economies. First, there has been a continuing shift from production of goods to production of services. The goods-producing sectors – agriculture and manufacturing – accounted for 35 per cent of the GDP of the industrialised economies during the 1960s. This proportion declined to less than 30 per cent in the mid-1980s, while the share of services expanded. Second, the use of traditional raw materials per unit of output has been declining. For instance, the average weight of cars made in the United States declined from 1700 Kg. in 1975 to 1500 Kg in 1985, and their iron and steel content declined by 12 per cent.[4] Technological innovations have led to economy in the use of materials. On these two counts the use of primary products per unit of GDP has declined.[5] In the foreseeable future, it would be unrealistic to expect the trade in raw materials to grow at anything like their rates during the 1950s and the 1960s. The growth in LDCs' share in the value of world export of manufactured goods made an important contribution to raising their overall share of world exports, especially since the second half of the 1970s. Their performance in this respect was particularly strong, and the exports of manufactures from LDCs increased faster than the world average. There is a large diversity in performance from country to country, which will be discussed later. Unlike trade in fuel products, where growth in the value of exports was due almost entirely to the unit price increase, there was a steady expansion in the volume of LDC trade in manufactures. For the first time in 1986 LDCs earned more from the exports of manufactures than from agriculture and mining.[6] Between 1980 and 1986 the share of manufactures in their total exports doubled, touching the 40 per cent mark[7] in 1986. This is trade in products ready to be sold in stores on the other side of the world. The products exported are mostly labour-intensive, ranging from clothes, shoes, transistor radios, digital watches, electrical and electronic appliances, television games, to intermediate manufactures, motorcycles, automobiles, and other transport equipment.

The industrial market economies continue to remain by far the largest markets for LDC exports, albeit the share of these

Table 1.2   VALUE AND VOLUME OF EXPORTS FROM DEVELOPING COUNTRIES

Year	Value in $ billion		Index of volume (1975 = 100)	
	Total	Manufactures	Total	Manufactures
1963	32	3.0	NA	NA
1973	100	24.0	NA	NA
1975	210.0	31.6	100	100
1976	254.2	42.2	118	134
1977	289.5	50.3	120	145
1978	300.2	63.4	124	160
1979	412.2	82.5	127	182
1980	553.9	100.3	112	199
1981	538.4	112.8	106	239
1982	481.3	111.8	99	242
1983	442.7	122.9	101	278
1984	458.7	147.3	107	345
1985	438.0	150.0	107	360

Source   GATT, *International Trade 1985–86*, Geneva, 1986, and the UNCTAD Secretariat data.

markets in total LDC exports fell from an average of 71 per cent for 1963–73 to 63 per cent in 1983. The industrial economies imported 67 per cent of LDC exports in 1985 as well as in 1986.[8] Between 1981 and 1985 the total exports of LDCs to industrial market economies declined by one-fifth. The declining trend continued in 1986. On this count, there were variations in regional experiences, reflecting *inter alia* differences in the intensity of efforts to achieve external adjustment and in the incidence of economic recovery in the industrialised countries. It also reflected the surge of protectionist measures in several large importing countries and the decline in the value of the dollar.

During the nineteenth century LDCs' trade links with the industrial countries (*à la* Irving Kravis) did not serve as an 'engine of growth' for the peripheral countries. However, a strong external demand for a country's exports does help and international trade did serve as a 'handmaiden' of successful growth.[9] During the postwar decades world trade and output growth were brisk, with trade growing one-and-a-half times to almost twice as fast as the average annual growth in world production. Over the period 1950–70 average world trade growth was 8.1 per cent a year, while merchandise production rose by 5.5 per cent per year. However, during the 1971–86 period the average rate of growth of world trade was halved, to 4.2 per cent and merchandise output growth slowed to 3.2 per cent a year.

Thus, trade did serve as a locomotive for the world economy during the 1950–70 period. This can certainly not be said about the succeeding period of 1971–86. The locomotive theory means that trade growth feeds back to stimulate production. By a wide margin, economic growth was higher in the decades of the 1960s and 1970s than in any other significant period of this century. These statistics show: (1) that since the early 1970s the average rate of growth of world output has declined; and (2) that growth has become less trade-intensive. The causes of this can be seen in the characteristics of this period, which was marked by resort to bilateral quantitative restrictions, market sharings arrangements, escalating subsidies and creeping protectionism in the world economy.

Another noteworthy feature is that the trade dependence of the developing economies has increased over the last three decades. Their exports, expressed as a share of GNP, experienced a sharp rise from 13 per cent in 1960 to 30 per cent in 1980. Although the growth in volume of trade for the LDCs has been notable, it is still a small part of the total world trade. In 1985 the merchandise exports of LDCs stood at 22.9 per cent of total world exports. In 1986 this proportion was 19.5 per cent, the lowest since 1970. The merchandise export statistics include engineering, chemicals, textiles and clothings, iron and steel, food, other primary products and fuels.

4   THE INTRA-TRADE

The share of developing countries' mutual trade has been growing along with industrialisation and economic growth in these countries. Between 1955 and 1971 intra-trade increased in value terms but decreased in terms of its share of world trade. However, between 1971 and 1981 it recorded a faster growth rate; in fact, it was higher than that for the trade of the rest of the world. Although it expanded, there has been no major shift towards trade among LDCs, at least when the focus is on the non-fuel merchandise trade, and the LDCs are defined to exclude the capital-surplus, oil-exporting developing countries. Between 1963 and 1973 the proportion of non-fuel exports remained stable at between 22.0 and 23.0 per cent of their total exports; thereafter it rose marginally to 24.0 per cent between 1975 and 1977. This stability is somewhat misleading, since at a more disaggregated level there have been opposing and mutually cancelling trends in trade in manufactures and primary commodities.

During the 1960s and 1970s manufactured exports were the most dynamic export sector of LDCs. Havrylyshyn and Wolf noted that the direction of these exports changed dramatically. In the late 1960s and early 1970s it was the industrialised countries that were the main recipients of an increased share of LDCs' manufactured exports. In the second half of the 1970s it was the capital-surplus oil-exporting developing countries whose share rose steadily.[10] The steep rise in the value of intra-trade over the 1970s hides increased oil prices.

With the help of the GATT data, Lall studied the period 1973
through 1981. The GATT data have a wider geographical
coverage than those used by Havrylyshyn and Wolf. The share
of non-oil LDCs in total manufactured exports rose briskly
during this period. Of this, the share of intra-trade was 28.5 per
cent in 1981; the industrial market economies recorded a
decline in their share. Even more interesting, of the 8.8 percentage points increase in the share of the LDCs during this period,
the OPEC countries accounted for 4.1 points and the non-oil
exporting LDCs for 4.7 points.[11] Thus, the oil-importing LDCs
displaced OPEC as the most dynamic market for the LDCs'
manufactured exports. Several LDCs – in particular the middle-
income ones – were able to develop a diversified industrial base
and expand their ability to supply a broad range of manufactured products.

As seen in Table 1.3, the intra-trade peaked in 1981. The
1981–86 decline was both in terms of value and the share in
world trade. Over this period the share of intra-LDC trade in
world trade declined from 7.8 per cent to 5.7 per cent. The
value of intra-trade in the mineral fuels declined by 46 per cent,
whereas that in other merchandise fell by 27.5 per cent.
Intra-trade in textiles and apparel declined, and so did the trade
in manufactures. Having peaked in 1981, the value of intra-
trade in manufactures stabilised around $42.5 billion.

An amber signal is warranted at this point. All the data are
expressed in current prices in United States dollars. Conse-
quently, the depreciation of commodity prices considerably
affected the overall results. While the volume index of exports
of the LDCs fell by only 5 per cent, the corresponding decrease
in the unit value of exports was some 15 per cent. The decline
should, therefore, be seen as a result of developments in the
world economy, rather than as a decrease in economic co-
operation among the LDCs. Another pointer in the same
direction is the annualised rate of decline. Intra-LDC trade for
the period 1981/82 to 1984/85 decreased by 2.9 per cent per
annum, whilst LDCs' exports to the industrialised world during
the same period fell at an annual rate of 5.2 per cent.[12]

The intensification of intra-trade in manufactures has led to a
structural change, in that the exports of manufactures have
become less dependent upon markets in industrialised countries. The shares of food and agricultural raw materials – the

Table 1.3   INTRA-LDC TRADE
(In $ Billion)

| | Merchandise Trade | | | |
	Fuels	Non-Fuels	Total	Manufactures
1970	3.8	7.2	11	3.4
1973	8.6	14.4	23	6.9
1979	46.4	51.6	98	30.5
1980	71.5	65.5	137	40.1
1981	78.3	70.7	149	45.5
1982	74.1	65.9	140	43.0
1983	63.9	64.1	128	42.3
1984	57.2	67.8	125	44.2
1985	52.9	63.1	116	40.7
1986	42.6	65.4	108	41.8

Source   GATT, *International Trade 1986–87*, Geneva, 1988.
Appendix II, various tables.

traditional exports of LDCs – in intra-trade have steadily declined. This is the outcome of a shift by LDCs to industrial production. The LDCs that emerged initially as exporters of labour-intensive manufactures, have gradually diversified their exports to more sophisticated and technology-intensive products. Some areas, however, have suffered a decline. For instance, mutual trade in textiles and clothing recorded a sharp fall. This was due to the fact that in many LDCs industrialisation began with the textile industry in response to internal demand. There was a small decline in the non-ferrous metals, partly because of the lowering of their prices, and partly because LDCs upgraded the processing of their raw materials. Although chemicals, other semi-manufactures and other consumer goods are still a major part of the mutual trade in manufactures, they have not shown any trend toward expansion.[13]

As for the structure of trade among LDCs, between 1970 and 1981 an increasing proportion of food items exported from the LDCs was destined to other LDCs – the proportion increased from 16.0 to 28.1 per cent. Since 1981 this share has virtually

stabilised. For cereals, however, the share has increased from
45.9 per cent in 1981 to 62.9 per cent in 1985, and for animal
and vegetable oils from 50.4 to 58.5 per cent. In 1985 35 per
cent of all food items imported by LDCs originated in other
LDCs. As seen in Table 1.3, there was a plunge in intra-trade in
manufactures in 1985. This set-back was particularly pro-
nounced in chemicals, textile yarns, and, to a lesser extent, in
passenger vehicles. According to the 1985 trade statistics LDCs
meet 82 per cent of the mineral fuels demand of the other
LDCs; in clothing this proportion is 44.1 per cent, 34.6 per cent
in non-ferrous metals, and 32.5 per cent in textile yarns. The
reversal in the intra-trade trend was caused by (1) the LDCs
whose real import demand was affected by debt servicing
stresses, (2) plummeting commodity prices and high inflation
rates (as in Latin America), (3) slower rate of growth and
decrease in the demand for development inputs (as in Africa), or
(4) the LDCs which increasingly oriented their exports towards
the markets of the industrialised countries (as in South and
South-East Asia).[14]

What does the future hold? Strant made a cross-country
model of non-fuel manufactured exports and statistically fitted
it to 1970–72 and 1976–78 data for 78 market economies.[15]
His broad conclusion was that the growth in intra-LDC trade
can be expected to continue far into the future. In particular, the
industrialised economies will continue to lose their share of
world trade in manufactures, and the LDCs will gain at their
expense. His projections suggest that by 1987 LDCs' share
would rise to 14 per cent of the total trade in manufactures, and
by 1997 to 21 per cent. By the year 2000, LDCs might well
supply one-fourth of the total traded manufactured goods.

Japan's experience in this regard is enlightening because it has
stayed on the middle rung between developed and developing
countries for several decades. Amsden compared the commodity composition of Japanese exports for the period 1929–71 and
found that as its GDP increased, the percentage of Japanese
exports destined to LDCs declined from a high of 82 per cent in
1929 to a low of 46 per cent in 1971. Further, although all
commodities exported from Japan before 1960 were highly
oriented towards LDCs, among them the SITC categories 6 and
8 became reoriented towards industrial countries over time. The
SITC 6 and 8 consist of textiles and apparel, and consumer

goods like medical products, cosmetics, cleaning products, electrical appliances and other miscellaneous manufactured goods. The lesson for the LDCs is that the commodity composition of a country's exports has an important bearing on directionality.[16]

Likewise, Maizels found that Canada exported 64 per cent of its SITC 6 and 8 exports to developing countries between 1929–57.[17] Like Japan, Canada's exports directed towards LDCs declined from a high of 77 per cent in 1929 to 36 per cent in 1955. Both for Japan and Canada, the declining trends indicate – as Staffan Linder would have suggested – that exports to LDCs prepare the way for exports to the industrialised countries.

The moral of the Japanese and Canadian stories is that the LDCs, especially the NICs, are under-exporting to each other. The two most industrialised areas, namely Latin America and South and South-East Asia, have low mutual trade. Their volume of mutual trade exhibits the ancient pattern of exchange between a Ricardian goods exporter (Latin America) and a Heckscher-Ohlin goods exporter (South and South-East Asia).

Several effective barriers to intra-trade exist; some of them are natural while others are policy-induced. First, the cost of transport, communications and other financial and currency clearing arrangements is said to be higher for intra-trade.[18] The oligopolistic pricing mechanism of the shipping conferences works unfavourably for LDCs. The scale economies are an important factor in the cost of communications and financial services. Only increased trade would increase their utilisation and bring the cost down. Thus, the relationship is circular. Second, inadequate (or missing) marketing channels like the large retailers, specialised import houses, and wholesalers, make it difficult for the intra-trade to grow beyond a rudimentary level. Third, the LDCs are known for highly protectionist trade regimes. Such commercial policies are another major hinderance. High tariff barriers would divert the flow of trade towards those countries which have low tariff walls.

The first benefit of intra-trade is the usual one, namely, the expansion of LDC trade, over and above their trade with other countries. The trade expansion allows reduction of production constraints associated with the small-sized domestic markets of many LDCs, stimulation of greater competition, scale-economies leading to lower prices, increased specialisation leading to industrial development, diversification of risk, and so on.[19] Secondly, the Heckscher-Ohlinian considerations would go into determining the pattern of the intra-trade. Some LDCs, that have successfully accumulated more physical and human capital, would be able to make a special niche for themselves on the international trade scene. These LDCs would have one kind of trade pattern with countries having a higher capital/labour ratio than themselves, and quite another kind with those having a lower capital/labour ratio. They would export labour-intensive goods to the former group of countries and physical-plus-human-capital-intensive goods to the latter. The observed trend is that the developing countries have exported mostly consumer goods and less sophisticated manufactures to industrialised market economics, and capital equipment and other technology-intensive products (like heavy equipment, construction material, transport equipment, motor vehicles, machines and metal products) mostly to developing countries. From this, one can infer that the intra-developing country trade can potentially provide a larger market for diversified trade.

In view of the creeping protectionism in the industrialised economies, the LDC markets acquire added significance. One group of economists contends that, given the uncertain – if not gloomy – prospects, more intensive mutual co-operation among LDCs will be necessary.[20] In terms of endowments, production structures and the level of growth, there is a great deal of diversity among developing countries. By intensive mutual co-operation and trade, they can exploit the complementarity of their different resource endowments and production facilities.

As for the welfare implications of intra-trade, there is little evidence that exports to LDC markets are superior to those to the other markets. At the same time it must be emphasised that there is no contradiction between intra-trade and exports to the industrialised world, that is, as long as the latter are not sacrificed to promote the former.

5   THE NICs AND THE LDC TRADE IN MANUFACTURES

Since over 60 per cent of the total merchandise trade is in manufactures, they dominate world trade. In the past three decades a restructuring of world industry and trade has taken place along with the tripling of manufactured output. Rapid growth was accompanied by a shift of manufacturing activity away from the old industrial centres to the newly developed countries and some LDCs. *Pari passu* with structural change, economic growth brought about changes in the comparative advantage, leading to shifts in the composition of output and eventually in the pattern of exports. In the dynamic continuum of economic growth, some LDCs have moved faster than others. The emergence of a sub-set of LDCs, namely, the newly industrialising countries (NICs), as fast growing exporters of manufactures is a part of the changing world economic structure. The emergence of NICs, thus, is not an isolated phenomenon. It accords with the necessary pattern of shift in the comparative advantage between countries as they move forward on the growth path.

The developing countries that implemented export-oriented growth strategies, in the latter half of 1960s, achieved higher rates of growth of manufactured exports. It is because of the NICs that the aggregate LDC share of world manufactured exports rose from 4.0 per cent in 1960 to 5.0 per cent in 1970, 9.7 per cent in 1980 to 12.1 per cent in 1985. It dipped marginally to 11.8 per cent in 1986. The share of manufactures in the total exports of the LDCs increased from 18 per cent in 1980 to 33 per cent in 1984 and 40 per cent in 1986. The NICs saw their share of world exports grow from 3.7 per cent in 1973 to 8.3 per cent in 1985, and in the process, they also became high growth export markets for the industrialised countries. The exports of manufactures of LDCs increased not only faster than the world average, but – as seen in the table below – faster than those from the industrial market economies.

The country performances in this regard have been highly diverse. Ten LDCs accounted for about 80 per cent of the total exports of manufactures in 1985. The most dynamic in this regard were the four East Asian NICs, namely Hong Kong, Korea (Republic of), Taiwan and Singapore. These economies

Table 1.4   GROWTH OF EXPORTS OF MANUFACTURES
(Annual Averages)

(In per cent)

	1965–70	1971–80	1981–85
Industrial Market Economies	13.4	18.7	0.4
Less Developed Countries	17.8	23.7	6.0

Source   United Nations, *World Economic Survey*, 1987, p. 59.

have become not only significant sellers but also significant buyers of manufactures on the world markets. For instance, as a group they accounted for 8 per cent of world exports and 5.5 per cent of world imports of manufactures in 1986.[21] Meanwhile, on-going industrialisation in other LDCs has set them on the path of expanding trade in manufactures. Other Asian countries, with lower labour costs, have started to capture the cheap, high-volume end of the markets. Malaysia and Thailand both started exporting cars in 1987. China is producing black-and-white televisions which were the staple of the Korean electronics industry until a few years ago.[22] Peru and the Philippines have also recorded impressive growth rates in industrial production. The degree of concentration of industrial production, therefore, should soon be diluted.

In contrast with the post-1971 years, the 1950–70 period was one of substantial growth and expansion in the OECD countries. The shift to outward-looking growth policies for the purpose of the fuller exploitation of comparative advantage in the NICs began in the early 1960s. The success of this policy package was facilitated by the economic environment in the OECD countries during that period. The NICs started competing with the industrial economies in their markets; they soon came to acquire a cutting competitive edge in several product lines, which inspired apprehension regarding the role of the NICs in some industrial economies during the post-1971 period.[23] This is attributable to two factors: first, in the industrial market economies, this was the beginning of a period of slow growth, high unemployment, adverse balance of payment pressures and huge exchange rate movements, followed by historically high interest rates. The simultaneity of problems inhibited the process of structural adjustment and revived protectionism; second, in some quarters in the industrial economies, the emergence of some LDCs capable of a dynamic manufactured export growth was seen as the beginning of a trend towards rapid industrialisation of LDCs. The lurking doubt was that it would eventually dampen – even disrupt – the industrial growth and exports of the industrial economies.

To qualify as a NIC, an LDC should have 20 per cent or higher share of its gross national product coming from the manufacturing sector. Yet there are as many as five different categorisations of the NICs by different international organisations. These classifications necessarily overlap each other, some more, some less. The one followed by the OECD secretariat is as follows:

Latin America	1.	Mexico
	2.	Brazil
Europe	3.	Portugal
	4.	Spain
	5.	Greece
	6.	Yugoslavia
Asia	7.	Korea (Republic of)
	8.	Taiwan
	9.	Hong Kong
	10.	Singapore

Source OECD, *The Impact of Newly Industrialising Countries on Production and Trade in Manufactures* (Paris: 1979).

Bradford, however, presents a variant of the above categorisation with a refinement. He followed a stages approach and classified them into the two-tier system opposite.

The four East Asian NICs were initially not taken seriously because they had fewer resources, lower starting economic levels and shorter industrial experience. But after the crises and the recessions of the 1970s subsided, it was clear that they were the most dynamic and the most resilient of the lot. Their exports are the largest in volume, followed by Brazil. The other first

	The First Tier NICs	The Second Tier NICs
East Asia	1. Taiwan 2. South Korea 3. Hong Kong 4. Singapore	1. Malaysia 2. Thailand 3. The Philippines 4. Macao 5. Indonesia
Latin America	5. Brazil 6. Mexico 7. Argentina	6. Colombia 7. Jamaica 8. Venezuala 9. Uruguay 10. Trinidad and Tobago
Africa		11. Tunisia 12. Morocco 13. Bahrain 14. Senegal 15. Ivory Coast
South Asia	8. India	16. Pakistan 17. Bangladesh

SOURCE   Bradford, Colin, I., 'The Rise of the NICs as Exporters on a Global Scale', in L. Turner and N. McMuller (eds.), *The Newly Industrialising Countries: Trade and Adjustment* (London: Allen & Unwin, 1982).

generation NICs, namely Mexico, Argentina and India do not loom as large in the gobal trade in manufactures as do the East Asians and Brazil. The four East Asian NICs and Brazil are also the most interesting from the point of view of understanding the NIC phenomenon. For them, trade policy has, indeed, played a part. Import-substitution was a common policy in the initial stages of economic and industrial growth. The five super-achievers had, in the later stage, taken a policy turn towards the outward-oriented trade policy, which accelerated their growth rates.

Casual empiricism suggests that the larger NICs, namely Argentina, Brazil and Mexico, with relatively high physical capital investment per capita, tend to have significantly larger exports of capital-intensive goods. Conversely Hong Kong, South Korea and Taiwan have relatively higher indexes of investment in human capital, and a greater proportion of their manufactured exports are in clothing, footwear and other consumer goods, and in standardised intermediate goods, which are more labour- and skill-intensive than the capital goods.[24] Hong Kong and Taiwan also export the highest proportion of consumer engineering goods. Their exports reflect the skill-intensity of their resource endowment and accord with the Heckscher-Ohlinian theoretical premise.

The second tier NICs reached the threshold of industrialisation later, and their industrial structure is not as firmly established as those of the first tier NICs. They have a relatively lower percentage of capital goods and consumer engineering exports. All their manufactured exports originate from those industries which need low investment in physical and human capital. This export pattern is in keeping with their resource endowment, and relies on heavy use of unskilled labour.[25] Most of their exports of finished products go to the industrial countries, but they are still relatively small in volume and are not tailored so well as to concentrate on specific export markets as those of the first tier NICs. Therefore, changes in the regional structures of exports are more likely to come from the second tier NICs than from the first.

2 The Link: Trade Policy and Economic Growth

1 THE VERACITY OF THE LINK

The question of the trade-growth nexus is complex, yet so fascinating and significant that it has rarely ceased to attract the attention of economic theorists, trade analysts and the policy-making community. Inevitably, therefore, it has drawn into its fold some of the sharpest minds of each generation of economists, ranging from Adam Smith and David Ricardo of the classical period, to J. S. Mill and Alfred Marshall of neo-classical times, to Dennis Robertson, Ranger Nurkse, Raul Prebisch, Jacob Viner and Arthur Lewis of more recent times, and to Balassa, Bhagwati, Krueger, Michaely and Riedel of the current period.

In the early 1950s Nurkse, Myrdal and Prebisch were the leading lights of the postwar challenge to the liberal trading and payments order. As expounded in Chapter 1, they were pessimistic about the future availability of trading opportunities to the LDCs. In keeping with the dominant Keynesianism of their period their arguments were based on the demand factor. The 'elasticity pessimism' originated during this period. The three proponents of this theory did not expect LDCs to export manufactures, and laid the foundations for import-substitution regimes.

The economic history of the past four decades does not bear out the predictions of the trade pessimists. History has sided with economists like Krueger[1] and Cairncross,[2] who were the foremost critics of export pessimism. Among the developing countries the richest region in 1950, namely Latin America, which followed an import-substitution policy regime, grew more slowly than the second poorest region, East Asia. Outward oriented strategies paid off for the latter country group, enabling it to change the life style of its people in the time span of one generation. A revealing comparison is that between Korea (Republic of), Egypt and India. In 1950 Korea

(Republic of) and Egypt had about the same population, and in terms of GNP per capita Korea was poorer than both Egypt and India. Its agricultural sector accounted for four-fifths of its GDP; it was a land of peasant farmers with per capita income of $450 (in 1987 dollars). In 1987 its per capital income was $2900. The comparable figures for Egypt and India were $610 and $270, respectively.

The 'Engine of Growth' Hypothesis

In the catchy phrase of Dennis Robertson, international trade was taken for an autonomous 'engine of growth'. As this mechanistic metaphor implies, trade and growth were thought to be connected by 'gears' whose tightness of fit determines the efficiency of the engine. Presumably there are two gears: the first links growth in LDCs to trade, that is, investment in LDCs depends upon imported capital goods. The second links the trade of LDCs to growth and economic prosperity in the industrialised countries.[3] The validity of this hypothesis rests on the tightness of the fit of the two principal 'gears'. The first of the two 'gears' can not be taken seriously because it is not only the LDCs which are reliant on imports of capital goods but small industrialised countries also depend on imported intermediate and capital goods. Although the second 'gear' does work, its quantitative significance can be judged from the fact that during the postwar period LDCs have grown more rapidly than the developed countries, on whose growth they are supposedly dependent.

During Robertson's era the world was simple and could be divided into primary commodity producing LDCs and the industrialised West. However, as set forth in Chapter 1, LDCs, particularly the NICs, have industrialised at an extraordinary pace, ending the simple dichotomy of previous years. The NICs export a diverse range of manufactures and successfully compete with those from the industrialised economies. The 'trade engine', therefore, no longer works in the same old way as was visualised. Yet work it does. In what way? That we shall see in the following sections.

Various Studies and their Implications

Nurkse raised the question of an optimal trade and development strategy for the postwar LDCs, and several economists of
note attempted to answer it using various analytical techniques.
Admittedly, from a methodological standpoint it is difficult to
examine the relationship between the openness to trade with the
outside world and the growth rate of an economy. It is no easy
task to formulate a model which, *ceteris paribus*, isolates the
impact of trade on the growing economy. There are other
determinants of growth like the structure of the national
product, domestic savings rate, capital stock, technological
influx and absorption, the ICOR, the quality of the labour force
and the macroeconomic policy line taken by the economy; all
would have a discernible influence on growth. Most models do
not filter their effects. Isolating the effects of these variables
required a general equilibrium approach, which is cumbersome
and sprawling in an econometric sense. To this end, several
economists have attempted to devise and refine techniques, but
there is no universally agreed upon method of quantifying and
isolating the contribution of any one factor to the growth rate.
Most scholars, therefore, use simple, partial equilibrium
models, some of which do yield telling results.

Without going into an exhaustive literature survey, by reviewing only the relevant literature one can find sufficient
cumulative evidence suggesting that the economies more open
to world trade have higher GNP growth rates. Several cross-
country studies have found a close and strong positive association between the growth of exports and that of GNP over the
last three decades. As for the question of the optimal proportion
of trade in the GNP of an LDC, one cannot find a simple
numerical answer, because of the so-called 'small country' and
'large country' effects. The optimal proportion must vary across
countries, depending upon the size of the LDC's economy and
the state of its natural resource endowment. For instance, South
Korea and Taiwan undoubtedly have to have a higher optimal
share of exports and imports in GNP, than a large resource-rich
LDC like Argentina or Brazil – assuming that the two sets of
LDCs are at the same income level. It is, therefore, wellnigh
impossible to prescribe a single number as an export growth

rate, or as a proportion of trade in GNP, which would pull an LDC out of the economic doldrums.

There are five major research projects which made cross-country estimates of the role of exports in economic growth. The techniques of estimation differed, so did the countries covered and the time horizon of the observations. Yet their conclusions are identical. The first study was that of Michalo-poulos and Jay,[4] which formulated a neo-classical production function with domestic capital, foreign capital and labour as inputs. They fitted the function with data for 39 LDCs for the decade of 1960s. Next, they re-estimated the coefficients after including exports as an additional independent variable. This study found that exports were highly significant and that they significantly improved the fit of the equation. It concluded that the growth rate of GNP and the growth rate of exports are highly correlated with each other.

The second study was undertaken by Michaely,[5] who esti-mated the relationship between the change in the proportion of exports in the GNP, and the rate of change in GNP. The first variable helped in eliminating the bias resulting from the fact that an increase of one unit of export is an increase of one unit in GNP. The sample comprised 41 LDCs while the time period was 1950–73. Michaely computed a Spearman rank correlation between the two variables; it was 0.38, and was significant at the 1 per cent level. Michaely also reported positive association of the economy's growth rate with the growth rate of the share of exports in GNP. It was observed to be particularly strong among the more developed LDCs, but did not exist among the least developed countries. This indicates that growth is affected by export performance only once countries achieve some mini-mum level of development.

The third estimate was the product of the wide-ranging US National Bureau of Economic Research (NBER) project on foreign trade regimes and economic development. These studies were done for ten LDCs for the period ranging from 1953 to 1973. The period varied from country to country, depending upon the availability of comparable data. The observations of GNP across countries were fitted on a pooled time-series cross-section basis. The GNP growth rate for each country was, thus, regressed against a time trend in that country's growth rate and the rate of growth of its exports. For the countries covered, it was observed that an increase in the rate of growth of export earnings of 1 percentage point annually was associated with an increase in the rate of growth of GNP of 0.1 percentage point.[6] Thus, the results were, once again, strongly indicative of a positive link between export growth and the overall growth rate.

The fourth major research attempt was made by Bela Balassa, who took data for 11 countries and re-estimated the Michaely relations, incorporating also the Michalopoulos-Jay factors of production.[7] His results conform to the ones arrived at by Michaely and Michalopoulos-Jay. He also noted the similarity in his results with those arrived at in Krueger's comprehensive NBER study.

Based on the actual factor accumulation paths, Balassa also showed that the increase in Korea's GNP would have been 37.0 per cent smaller if its export growth had equalled the average for the LDCs in the sample. The corresponding proportion was 25.0 per cent for Taiwan. At the other end of the spectrum, in Chile, India and Mexico, respectively, the increase in GNP would have been 14.0, 12.0 and 8.0 per cent greater if these countries had had the average export growth rate of the sample LDC group.

Fifth, Foder worked with a sample of 19 LDCs. With the help of 31 observations he provided evidence supporting the hypothesis that export-oriented policies both led the economy to an optimal allocation of resources and generally enhanced productivity.[8] He also found a positive correlation between exports and GNP growth. The estimates show that there are, on average, substantial differences in marginal factor productivities between the export and non-export sectors. These differences derive in part from the failure of entrepreneurs to equate marginal factor productivities and are in part due to externalities. The latter are generated because the export sector imparts positive effect to productivity in the non-export sector.

To this must be added the results of a recent study (Chow, 1987) that goes into the causal relationship between export growth and industrial development. This study took a sample of eight NICs to perform the Sims' causality test. Most of the 32 regression equations that were estimated have relatively high R-square values. The findings implicitly support the hypothesis that a causal relationship exists between export growth and industrial development.[9] Except for Argentina, export growth has significantly influenced the process of industrial development. It is indicated by the unidirectional causality in Mexico and by bidirectional causality in Hong Kong, Israel, Korea, Singapore and Taiwan. Even for Brazil, which has a relatively large domestic market, export growth has a bidirectional causal link with the development of the manufacturing sector. Argentina was the only exception. These results further confirm the advantage of an export-oriented growth strategy.

A caveat would be in order: all these studies, except Chow's, imply only a positive association between the degree of openness of the economy and GNP growth, that is, they confirm a statistical relationship between export and income growth. But association cannot be taken for causation. Also, these studies provide only stylised facts, not a theory. An underlying theoretical model is needed for making causal inferences, whose validity can then be tested by standard econometric techniques.

The results of the statistical works cited above are supported by several recent studies, including those which extended the time period analysed through the economically disturbed period of the 1970s. For example, a World Bank study compared not only the growth performance of LDCs pursuing different trade strategies, but also their ability to withstand external shock.[10] Like the other studies, it established a robust relationship between the growth of exports and the GNP of 43 sample LDCs.[11] In addition, it indicated that LDCs following free-trading macroeconomic policies – having no bias against exports – succeeded in maintaining higher GDP growth rates during the period of exogenous shocks as well, that is, the decade of the 1970s.

At the same time, the comparative studies of the effects of import substitution by Little, Scitovski and Scott demonstrated that these policies become less and less efficient if they are maintained for long periods.[12]

This is a vitally significant revelation for the policy professionals. There are two more recent country studies which corroborate in a qualitative manner the same conclusions of brisk economic growth following from a liberal free-trading macroeconomic policy regime, whereas a non-neutral and illiberal policy regime leads the economy in the opposite direction.

One of these was done by Tsiang (1985) on Taiwan,[13] and the other by Kim (1985) on South Korea.[14]

Using data from the *World Development Report, 1986*, on GDP, labour force growth, the growth of export and investment shares in GDP for 18 LDCs, Lall and Rajapatirana found that there was a positive and statistically significant association between income growth rates and growth of exports in GDP.[15] Like Balassa (1982), the time period chosen by them was the turbulent decade after the oil shock, that is, 1973–84.

The last word in this regard comes from Greenaway and Nam (1988), who deployed data for 41 developing countries which accounted for over 65 per cent of the total output of developing countries in 1985. Although the sample LDCs were non-random – the selection was influenced by data availability – they comprised a geographically diverse group, a range of countries at various stages of development and LDCs of different sizes. They classified these LDCs according to the orientation of their trade policy in the following groups: 'strongly outward-oriented', 'moderately outward-oriented', 'strongly inward-oriented', and 'moderately inward-oriented' economies.[16] To see whether export-orientation facilitates a more productive use of investible resources, each LDC group was examined for two sub-periods, 1963–73 and 1973–85. Table 2.1 relates to each LDC-group with the following indicators of macroeconomic performance: annual average growth rate of real per capita income, annual average growth rate of merchandise exports, average gross domestic savings rates, annual average ICOR and the average debt service ratio, which is measured in terms of the percentage of exports. For starters, taking the saving averages: as seen in Table 2.1, in 1963 the lowest ratio was recorded for the LDCs in sub-group A1, whilst those in A2 and B1 recorded ratios of 20 per cent or more and the LDCs in B2 15 per cent. Between 1963 and 1985 the ratios for A2 and B1 countries improved slightly and that for B2 increased by around 3 percentage points. In contrast, the ratio for A1 countries went up by two and a half times, from 13 to 31.4 per cent, which implies that the outward-oriented LDCs have been the most successful in marshalling investible resources. Increasing savings are not a sufficient condition for growth; for faster growth they should be utilised efficiently.

Table 2.1 MACROECONOMIC PERFORMANCE OF LDCs GROUPED BY THEIR TRADE ORIENTATION

Country development strategy	Average Annual Growth of Real GDP		Average Annual Growth of Real Per Capita GNP		Average Annual Growth of Merchandise Exports		Average Gross Domestic Savings Rate		Average Gross Foreign Savings Rate		Average Annual ICOR		Average Debt-Sav Ratio (Percent)	
	1963–1973	1973–1985	1963–1973	1973–1985	1965–1973	1973–1985	1963	1985	1963	1985	1963–1973	1973–1985	1970	1985
A1 Strongly outward-oriented	9.5	7.7	6.9	5.9	10.8	11.2	13.0	31.4	9.5	2.0	2.5	4.5	4.1	5.9
A2 Moderately outward-oriented	7.6	4.3	4.9	1.7	8.8	8.6	20.0	20.6	1.4	-2.3	2.5	5.0	7.5	20.9
A Outward-oriented (average)	7.9	5.0	5.2	2.5	9.4	9.8	19.0	23.4	2.5	2.3	2.5	4.9	6.2	13.5
B1 Moderately inward-oriented	6.8	4.7	3.9	1.8	14.1	5.5	22.9	24.1	1.7	2.2	3.3	6.2	11.3	29.0
B2 Strongly inward-oriented	4.1	2.5	1.6	-0.1	2.2	1.4	15.0	17.9	2.4	0.2	5.2	8.7	16.5	21.1
B Inward-oriented (average)	5.2	3.7	2.7	1.0	8.8	2.5	17.6	21.2	2.1	1.1	4.1	7.0	14.2	25.6

SOURCE Greenaway and Nam (1988). Table 3.

Examples of LDCs with high savings and low growth rates abound. India is perhaps the best illustration of growth failure despite a high savings rate. ICOR is one indicator of efficient use of investible resources–lower ICOR means less additional capital needed to produce an extra unit of output. For both the sub-periods, the ICORs of the outward-oriented economies were lower than those of the inward-oriented LDCs, with the gap between the two widening in the latter period. The implication is that investible resources have been more productively and effectively deployed in the outward-oriented developing economies. The saving and ICOR link is conspicuously mirrored in the GDP growth rates, and confirms the saving-investment-ICOR-growth causal link. The fastest growing economies have been the group A LDCs, between 1963–73 the real GDP grew at an annual rate of 9.5 per cent in the A1 sub-group, yielding a group average of 7.9 per cent. In the B1 and B2 sub-groups the growth rates were 6.8 and 4.1 per cent respectively, yielding a group average of 5.2 per cent. The differences continued over the 1973–85 period, and the highest growth rate was observed in group A1. Although during this period the growth rates declined in all the sub-groups, the proportionate decline was greater in the inward-oriented LDCs.

The real growth rates of merchandise exports were found to be highest in the sub-group B1 (14.1 per cent); then came A1 (10.8 per cent), A2 (8.8 per cent) and B2 (2.2 per cent) during 1965–73. Yet the group average was higher for the outward-oriented economies. The differences between the two groups became greater for the period 1973–85; the A1 sub-group increased its rate to 11.2 per cent whilst that for A2 fell marginally to 8.6 per cent. As opposed to this, the B1 rate collapsed and the B2 sub-group recorded an annual average rate of minus 1.4 per cent. The implication is that in the post oil-shock period, the outward-oriented economies recorded a much more impressive export performance than the inward-oriented ones.

Since the advent of the debt crisis, the ability to service debt has become an important and widely monitored indicator. It is of interest to know which group of LDCs is more successful in this regard. For 1970, one can observe that there is a monotonic escalation in the debt-service ratio from A1 to B2 sub-groups, with group averages being 6.2 per cent for the outward-oriented

LDCs, and 14.2 per cent for the inward-oriented LDCs. By 1985 the ratios had increased substantially for all the sub-groups. In A1, despite the inclusion of Korea, one of the world's largest LDC debtors, the ratio showed a minor increase. In all the other sub-groups the ratio increased to over 20 per cent, with the highest ratio being recorded in the B1 (29 per cent). The group averages in 1985 were 13.5 per cent for the outward-oriented economies and 25.6 per cent for the inward-oriented economies.

Notwithstanding the shortcomings, real income per capita is the most widely used measure of economic welfare in international and intertemporal comparisons. For the 1963–74 period, a clear declining trend of growth rates, from 6.9 per cent in A1 to 1.6 per cent in B2, is visible. During the 1973–85 period A1 recorded the highest growth rate and B2 the lowest, at minus 0.1 per cent. For both the periods the averages for the outward-oriented LDCs were substantially higher than those for the inward-oriented LDCs. Greenaway and Nam concluded that the above results show that capital formation and growth rates have been higher in the outward-oriented LDCs. Also, the ICORs have been lower, merchandise exports higher and the rate of per capita income growth higher in the same group of LDCs. The differences have been most marked between A1 and B2 sub-groups, and in some cases not so marked between A2 and B1 categories.

Thus higher growth and greater resilience of the economy appear to be related to the more even-handed or free-trade policy regime, or, as second best, an export-biased one. The hitherto unanswered question, however, is: why LDCs with superior export performance are also the LDCs with superior economic performance? Although the theory of optimal resource allocation does give part of the answer, it is certainly not the complete answer. There is more to it than that. There is no single, universally agreed upon diagnosis of the reasons for the difference in performance.

The policy-maker finds himself on the horns of a dilemma, because the economic theory indicates import substitution and export promotion should both be analysed in marginal terms. One additional unit of foreign exchange saved equals one additional unit of foreign exchange earned. So what to adopt, import substitution or export promotion? For a clear answer, let us analyse what happens under the two regimes and which one would have a more beneficial effect on a developing economy.

However, before going into that, it must be clarified that considerable confusion exists in the literature about what exactly is meant by 'export promotion' or 'export orientation' in trade regime. A precondition of export orientation is restoration of neutrality in the incentives to produce exportables, importables and non-traded goods. The neutral status for export activities in LDCs can be achieved by providing a combination of the following five elements: (1) a flexible and realistic exchange rate; (2) free trade in inputs and outputs; (3) competitive financial and money markets; (4) competitive primary input markets; and (5) non-discriminatory domestic taxes.[17] A neutral policy ensures that exports are not discouraged relative to import substitution. When the trend of export incentives is higher than that of those for import substitution, we say that the policy regime is export promoting or export oriented. For instance, if in addition to neutral status, the exporter is granted a tax incentive of 50 per cent of the world market value added, then the exporter would enjoy something like an effective protection rate of 50 per cent in contrast to an import-substituting firm.

The benefits of a neutral incentive structure come from an expansion of the most efficient import-substituting activities (for example, agriculture) rather than only expanding exports. Neutrality of incentives encourages the expansion of those activities which can save or earn foreign exchange at the lowest cost. Korea and Taiwan, for example, had heavily protective import substitution trade regimes in the 1950s, before they switched to outward-orientation in the early 1960s. This is when their gradual reduction in tariffs began and the two economies became known for their low protective barriers and economic distortions. Their export promotion strategy implies a more or less even-handed or neutral regime, without a bias against exports. This contrasts with the policy regime in a country like India, which has a discernible bias against exports.

The experience of the last two decades has been a source of lasting controversy and subject to varying interpretations by economists. Ranis[18] and Little[19] see the growth of the East Asian countries as the predictable result of freeing trade and removing discrimination against exports. But Diaz-Alejandro[20] and Streeten[21] stress that the active role of the government, well-honed human resources and favourable international environment are the special features behind the superior performance of the East Asian NICs. Notwithstanding the differing views, there is considerable common ground among economists debating trade and development strategies. There is general agreement that the degree of openness of an economy represents nothing but the size of gains from trade. Using the conventional neo-classical theory, it implies moving on to or close to the optimal point on the production possibility frontier. However, the static gains achieved in shifting to more efficient patterns of trade are not the most important reason for the high growth rates in the successful developing countries. Increased productivity is even more important. Identifying the virtues of outward-looking policies is thus only a starting point for unravelling the causal link between trade and economic growth.

2   THE ECONOMIC THEMES AT WORK

A comparison of economic performance under the two regimes would now be in order.

- An inward-looking strategy relies on the home market for manufactured products to the point of abandoning efforts towards an early conquest of foreign markets. Under this regime import substitution is promoted through tariffs, subsidies, quantitative restrictions, stringent exchange controls, licensing and similar control measure. Inflationary domestic policies are followed with only peripheral concern for their impact on international trade.

- Inward-oriented trade policies are known to strongly bias the system of incentives against exports, which leads to poor export performance and increasing restrictions on the trade and payments regimes. The result of this policy orientation is progressively diminishing export earnings, while imports have to be restricted to mere 'essentials', which in turn affects net investment both quantitatively and qualitatively.

- Although foreign exchange availability declines with the adoption of import substitution, the demand for imported goods and services remains the same – if it does not accelerate with the growth process. As imports of capital and intermediate goods have to continue, output and capital formation, even within the import substituting sectors, become dependent upon the availability of foreign exchange. A growing gap between demand and supply of foreign exchange has been the commonest feature of the LDCs adopting import substitution policies.

- Import substitution is *inter alia* the strategy for saving foreign exchange. Export promotion *inter alia* is the strategy for earning foreign exchange. In many import-substituting LDCs, increased dependence on imports and lagged foreign exchange earnings are reflected in periodic balance of payments crises. Scarcity of foreign exchange restricts output and becomes a binding constraint on the growth rate.

- In most LDCs, the domestic market is not large enough to support the development of a large number of industries at economic-scale production. After import substitution in low-technology industries, such as textiles, basic chemicals, light engineering products, and so on, where imports are initially sizeable, it appears that additional industries are generally established at uneconomically small sizes. Once the 'easy' stage of import substitution is completed, it has been observed that the incremental capital/output ratio rises at a steep rate, which tells on economic growth. By enlarging the market size, export promotion allows the benefits of economies of scale. This is an important factor contributing to economic growth because these benefits are costless.

- Countries that actively discriminate against foreign trade, by giving greater incentives to production for the domestic market, forgo the benefits of efficiency and permit poor macroeconomic policies to continue. They also fail to fully exploit their comparative advantage.

- A large bureaucracy is created to run the import–substitution regime. The proliferation of a control network in all its complexity seems to be another common feature of such a regime. The cumbersome nature of the instruments used leads to X–inefficiency and eventually results in tapering off of growth rates.

  In an outward-looking trade regime the role of the government or bureaucracy is relatively restricted. If governments are serious about exporting manufactures, their freedom to intervene is restricted by the exigencies of keeping manufactures internationally competitive and by trade conventions that limit permissible methods of trade promotion.

  Unproductive economic activities like rent-seeking become commonplace in an import-substituting regime. Rent-seeking embraces lobbying activities designed to capture the rents – that is, scarcity premiums – that are attached to licenses and quotas.

- LDCs following the import-substitution regime are known to have adopted effective protection rates of several hundred per cent. Protection is carried to extremes. Instances where the cost of imports for producing domestically exceed the import value of the final product are not unheared of. High cost, low-quality output persists under this regime.

- The quantitative restrictions under the import–substitution regime lead to a built-in tendency for relative prices to diverge from their optimum. The end result is that currencies tend to become increasingly overvalued, which adversely affects exports and results in inappropriate allocation of resources. On the other hand, LDCs adopting outward-looking trade policies are known to maintain appropriate and realistic exchange rates.

- Under the outward-oriented regime, if tariffs are applied, their rate is non-discriminatory. Also, to make local prices and wages appear cheap, anti-inflationary monetary and fiscal policies are consciously pursued.

- Import substitution precludes competition. The licensing system treats the successful, low-cost producers and the less successful, high-cost producers alike. The competitive market mechanism for weeding out the inefficient producers, and thereby raising average industrial productivity, is obstructed by regulations supporting the import-substitution strategy. An open economy would *a priori* promote internal competition and so greater economic efficiency. A degree of foreign competition is tolerated at home to toughen the competitive fibre of local industries. Besides, exposure to international competition is the best anti-monopoly policy in practice, and it prevents the development of high-cost industries.

- The phrase 'outward-looking' signifies constant and deliberate attention to industrial and trade developments outside the country. An important ingredient in this policy is a strong effort to remain in touch with and absorb the latest technology, and make endeavours to catch up with the industrialised economies. An import-substituting economy distances itself from the modern world outside. An example is India's computer hardware industry, in which import-substitution has resulted in higher costs, unavailability, and enormous lags in the use of computers in schools, tourism and the judiciary and myriad other walks of life. This is despite the fact that India has an educated population and skill-endowed economy. This policy regime has also inhibited the rapid adoption of modern information-technology-based processes, which are essential for enhancing efficiency and productivity in the industrial sector.

- An open, outward-looking developing economy is constantly influenced by international factors. This helps in bringing the incentives for domestic resource allocation closer to the international opportunity costs, and hence close to what would produce efficient results.

- A comfortable balance of payments position, resulting from successful exports, eases up the excesses of the import–substitution strategy.

- The two-gap theory demonstrates that under a foreign exchange bottleneck, additional foreign exchange earned by way of exports is more productive than under the savings bottleneck.

- An export-promotion strategy promotes the inflow of substantial non-aid foreign capital. Superior export performance raises the creditworthiness of the LDC and facilitates capital market borrowings.

- Export promotion attracts the transnational corporations to exploit Heckscher-Ohlin type factor-endowments in the host LDC. This leads to a second generation 'ripple effect' in economic growth.

- Under export-promotion regimes firms stay tuned to the market signals. Therefore, this regime, unlike its rival, facilitates rapid expansion of the least-cost firms and industrial sectors. In addition, it enables entry of the new firms at an economically efficient size.

- Export promotion strategy contributes to an economic dynamics in which a more efficient firm or industrial sector pushes out the less efficient one. Firms compete for market share and, thereby, keep in healthy shape by adopting the latest technology. Market is made into a tough place where only the fittest survive.

- An export-promotion strategy provides self-correcting mechanisms to align the macroeconomic variables that affect growth. For instance, if the exchange rate becomes overvalued, it is easily detected under an export-promotion regime because the trade balance goes into deficit. The misalignment can be detected under an import-substitution regime as well, but the signals are feeble. For instance, overvaluation of the currency can be indicated by a decline in premiums on import licenses.

These are the broad economic themes that seem to be at work. They bring us to the inference that there are cogent and convincing reasons for the economic performance of LDCs to be better under an export-promotion regime than under import−substitution, or when there is no discrimination against exports and the macroeconomic policies and the system of incentives are neutral. Little is known about how each of the above factors contributes to growth. It is likely that each of the phenomenon contributes, though in different degrees, in different LDCs. Thus, the contention that trade promotes growth and prosperity is as valid today as it was in 1817 when Recardo posited the classical theory of international trade.

3   ARE THERE LIMITS TO EXPORT EXPANSION?

The strong positive association between export performance and rapid growth as well as its plausible reasons have already been set forth. We have also seen the inefficiencies of import−substitution regimes documented by both the exhaustive NBER and OECD studies. But for an outward-looking strategy to succeed, market access in the importing countries is vitally important. As seen in Chapter 1, it was during the buoyant decades of the 1950s and 1960s that markets in the industrialised countries grew fast and readily absorbed the exports of the LDCs which had adopted an outward-looking trade strategy. During these decades the present−day NICs were able to expand their share in world trade. Stagflation, followed by recession, fuelled protectionist tendencies in the industrialised countries. The changed climate − so the argument goes − has darkened the prospects for the second wave of LDCs which are hoping to follow in the wake of the first-tier NICs.

Scepticism is rife about the prospects of other developing countries which are on the threshold of becoming second-tier

NICs. In general, while forecasting their exports, under-estimates are made by (1) focusing only on the known exports, and (2) having downward estimation biases in the price elastici-ties of such exports. Little wonder, economics has been popu-larly known as the dismal science. The principal proponent of this argument is Cline (1982), who raised doubts on the following two counts:

(1)   A general LDC adoption of an export-promotion stra-tegy would cause a spectacular increase in the pressure of LDC exports on industrialised country markets.
(2)   The industrialised countries would be politically unable to resist the resulting protectionist pressures.[22]

A priori these doubts seem plausible, but they do not stand up to close scrutiny. Firstly, LDCs cannot be seen as a monolithic bloc. Different LDCs have different endowments, and are at different stages of economic development. This implies that different LDCs would arrive at a substantial manufactured goods exports capacity at different points in time. Secondly, in the highly unlikely event of their all starting in this direction at the same point in time, they still produce goods with different attributes, and different capital/labour ratios. Thirdly, in keep-ing with the Heckscher-Ohlin theory, the majority of the LDCs are expected to maintain a strong raw material component in their exports. Fourthly, the majority of them are unlikely to start exporting like the present-day NIC any time in the immediate future. It is only the countries which are listed as the second generation NICs which display a high export potential in the medium term, or perhaps in the short term.

There are other persuasive reasons to prove the doubting Thomases wrong. Foremost, Cline made the mistake of putting all LDCs on a curve, duly adjusted, for the successful East Asian exporters, with very high ratios of trade to national income. But outward-looking strategy is not taken to mean that LDCs should go on an export binge and export as much as they can. It only implies having a neutral package of incentives, market liberalisation and eschewing policy discrimination against ex-ports. Second, industrialised countries are not the only markets to absorb increased LDC exports. The potential second–tier

NICs may vie for export markets in (1) the industrial countries, (2) the present NICs, and (3) the other middle-income LDCs. Trade policy changes in LDCs can enhance the volume of intra-trade; there are ample opportunities for opening new sectors such as agriculture and services to free trade. Besides, LDCs have started exporting textiles and apparel to Japan, and replacing Japan's exports of these products in other industrial— country markets. The second-tier NICs at this point have a five— to ten-year lag behind the present-day NICs, and the latter are moving increasingly into sophisticated engineering products,[23] leaving more product lines behind for the former. This is the spectacle of changing comparative advantage; both the commodity composition and factor content of exports changes with it. In addition, trade economists have increasingly appreciated the potential for intra-industry trade as trade opportunities are provided. Such intra-trade in manufactures among LDCs and between them and the developed countries can grow significantly. The experience in the EEC of increase in mutual trade in similar products with progressive dismantling of trade barriers is relevant in this regard.[24]

A policy shift in LDCs towards economic liberalism and open economies would spur the growth rates in the middle-income LDCs, which would yield a more than proportionate increase in the intra-LDCs trade. A large proportion of this trade would be in goods which cannot be exported to the industrial-country markets for quality reasons and those of taste. Also, a by-product of the adoption of an export promotion strategy by LDCs would be an opening up of their markets and, therefore, extra exports from the developed countries. Growth in per capita income would enable the LDCs to increase their imports from the industrialised countries.[25]

The limits-of-export-expansion argument implicitly assumes that in import/output (M/O) ratio, the numerator increases while the denominator is constant. A country can import all it consumes (let C = consumption), and the M/C ratio can range from 0 to 1.0. But the ratio of import to output is limitless; it is possible to import more than the output – some of it can be exported. This implies intra-industry trade – a phenomenon of high significance – which allows high trade-to-output ratios. There are, indeed, limits to this also, but they fall short of the belief that there is not enough absorptive capacity in the industrial countries for a surge of LDC exports. For the 1970s, the LDC imports-to-consumption ratio in the industrialised countries was calculated at between 1.7 and 2.4 per cent.[26] Even if there is a five-fold increase, it would mean a market penetration ratio by LDCs of between 8.5 and 12.0 per cent, which is way below the abstract 100 per cent limit.

The second conceptual weakness of export pessimism is that it ignores the income effect. It is not reasonable to say that a five-fold increase in exports would leave income unaffected. Havrylyshyn provides plenty of historical-analytical evidence, for the nineteenth century as well as the recent past, to support the view that dynamism in trade contributes to greater production.[27] If a computation is done for the first quarter of the last century, it would have appeared that relative to the 1850 base of world income, the erstwhile flood of exports from Europe could not be absorbed by Britain. In fact, the growth rates of exports after 1830 were far higher in the European economies than in Britain, and all their exports were absorbed in Britain. The same observation applies to Japan, the proto-NIC during the 1950s. Its astounding success in exports made it the original role model for the East Asian NICs. Using the Cline procedure, based on Chenery-Syrquin equations, for 1965, Havrylyshyn found that Japanese exports exceeded its norms by 1.56, compared to the 4.93 value Cline calculated for the East Asian NICs. Following the Japanese pattern, these NICs should have had export increases of only 2.6 times; in reality they grew far more than this during 1970–79 alone. These exports were easily absorbed with penetration ratios rising from 1.7 per cent to 3.4 per cent. Scepticism about the NICs not being able to match the performance of Japan could similarly have been raised at that point.

The proponents of this argument must know that international trade is more than mere exporting, and that LDCs wish to export more for one reason only, eventually to be able to import more. They cannot go on investing their trade surpluses in the international capital markets or adding to their international reserves. If not sterilised, enduring surpluses could set an inflationary spiral in motion in the exporting LDC economy and generate pressures for currency revaluation. The Japanese and Swiss economies are two recent examples of this phenomenon. Higher exports by LDCs necessarily implies greater imports by them, which are then additional exports for the industrial countries. This is simple, but cogent, logic in support of the feasibility of export expansion. Extra exports from the industrial countries to LDCs contribute to the GDP of the former. This occurs in a multiplicative way, both in the Keyensian sense of macro-stimulus and in the Schumpeterian sense of micro-entrepreneurial stimulus. Without taking a long-term, dynamic view of things, one is liable to reach a wrong policy decision. The long-term benefits of increased imports from LDCs would eventually lead to high export/GDP ratios in the industrialised countries. I hasten to add that it is not enough to dwell on the export/GDP ratio alone. What matters is the total trade-to-output ratios, not only imports or only exports.[28] This analysis convincingly debunks the limit-to-export-expansion thesis.

3 Developing Countries in the Multilateral Trading System

1 THE INITIATION

The General Agreement on Tariffs and Trade (GATT) was established on 30 October 1947, principally by the industrialised countries, which still dominate it because they dominate the international trading scene. Twenty-three countries were the original signatories of the GATT charter. The membership, however, has grown. Lesotho became a Contracting Party under Article XXVI of the General Agreement in January 1988, bringing GATT membership to 96. In addition, one country has acceded provisionally and a further 28 apply in practice the rules of GATT to their commercial policy.[1]

The developing countries did not have a meaningful role in drafting the GATT charter; it was, therefore, not dominated by development considerations. Presently, all the LDCs accounting for the bulk of LDCs' trade are the Contracting Parties of the GATT. For a long while, the stance taken by the LDCs in the GATT has been that in terms of economic strengths, trade volumes and market sizes, the Contracting Parties of the GATT are highly uneven. Therefore, in the international trading system, unequals must not be treated as equals. Premised on this belief, they sought and obtained a variety of 'special and differential treatment' measures for their products, notably through (1) relief from certain GATT obligations, and (2) the Generalised System of Preferences (GSP). It has, however, been debated how valuable the 'special and differential' measures have been for LDCs.

The interests of the developing countries were taken care of by Article XVIII of the GATT, which recognised that LDCs may need tariff flexibility, and some quantitative restrictions to conserve foreign exchange. They are also allowed to restrict

42

imports to protect their infant industries. Yet, by the early 1960s, there was a growing disillusionment with the gains which LDCs were making from the GATT system. Therefore, in 1965, a new chapter – Part IV – was added to the General Agreement, committing industrialised countries to assist the LDCs. It provided for freedom from the obligations to offer reciprocal concessions at the time of negotiated tariff reductions. The developed countries agreed that, except when compelling reasons made it impossible, they would refrain from increasing barriers to the exports of primary and other products of special interest to LDCs. They also agreed to give high priority to reducing existing barriers.

Further elaborations were subsequently made in the Tokyo Round (1973–79) agreement; the industrial economies agreed not to expect LDCs, in the course of trade negotiations, to make contributions inconsistent with their individual development, and financial and trade needs. Greater differential treatment was provided to LDCs in the area of subsidies and countervailing duties, technical barriers to trade, and customs valuation. A Committee on Trade and Development was also set up under the aegis of the GATT to ensure that the trade-related problems of LDCs receive priority attention. Its role was strengthened after the Tokyo Round by the creation of two new subcommittees: one to examine any new protective measures taken by the industrialised countries against imports from LDCs, and the other to consider the trade problems of the least-developed countries.

2 RELUCTANT MULTILATERAL PARTICIPATION

With a few exceptions, LDCs largely remained passive participants in the successive rounds of the Multilateral Trade Negotiations (MTNs). They took advantage of Article XVIII, and subsequently of the provisions of Part IV of the GATT code, and were unwilling to place themselves in situations where they might have been expected to make reciprocal tariff reductions. Under the available set of international trade regulations, LDCs succeeded in getting relief from the obligations of offering reciprocal concessions at various rounds of the MTNs. But the LDCs paid for this favouritism with weakened bargaining power. As a result, in the MTNs the bigger tariff cuts were on goods which matter least for LDCs' export earnings. They benefitted less than the countries which were full participants in the give and take of the MTNs.

At the time of the initial rounds of the MTNs, non–participation was forced on LDCs because not many had acquired the status of Contracting Party. Second, the bargaining process was such that due to small market sizes and narrow trade structures in LDCs, industrialised countries had little inclination to exchange tariff concessions with them. Third, the majority of LDCs had little experience of negotiating trade issues, which adversely affected the participation level of LDCs in the negotiations. They were reduced to mere sideline ob-servers. Nevertheless, the developing countries did benefit from the general trade liberalisation under the most-favoured-nation (MFN) principle. This uneven game, however, allowed their domestic economies to become highly controlled and tariff-ridden.

The failure of LDCs to participate and offer reciprocal tariff concessions during the MTNs contributed to a bias in tariff cuts away from the labour-intensive manufactured exports of LDCs. Finger has produced data on how US imports were affected during the Kennedy Round negotiations by the level of partici-pation by a group of countries.[2] It was observed that the lower the participation by a group of countries, the lower the share of imports from that group that benefitted from US concessions.

Country Group	Affected Imports as Percentage of Imports From Each Country Group
1. Major Participants	70
2. Other Developed Country Participants	49
3. Active Developing Country Participants	33
4. Other Developing Countries	5

3 THE GROWTH OF ILLIBERAL TRADE REGIMES IN LDCs

With some notable exceptions, like Hong Kong, Kuwait and Singapore, LDCs have traditionally relied heavily on tariff and non-tariff barriers to trade. Governments directly control all import transactions or canalise all bulk imports in most LDCs, with the poorest countries having the most restrictive trade regimes. Apart from the incidence of high statutory levels of tariff, it is the web of para-tariff measures – for example, foreign exchange licensing, special taxes on imports, import licensing and a myriad of quantitative restrictions (QRs) – that make the trade regimes in LDCs extremely illiberal. They are also characterised by considerable complexity and variability. Tariffs are not only high, they are seldom bound, and typically applied more erratically than those used by industrial countries. Producer goods, especially capital goods, being considered more essential than consumer goods, are generally less protected.

Primarily, it was balance of payments fears that lay at the root of most protective policies in LDCs, for which the foreign exchange 'gap' theory provided an *ex post* rationalisation. Secondly, during the initial period of their growth there was a justifiable slapping on of infant-industry-tariffs in the LDCs. But even after these infant industries matured, the high tariffs persisted and the resulting inefficiencies became all pervasive in their economic systems. In addition, many LDCs made the mistake of offering infant-industry protection to industries that never grew up to be internationally competitive.

The prolonged periods of illiberal domestic policy have impeded economic growth and structural transformation in most LDCs. Many of the welfare reducing influences are not even discernible to the untrained eyes. By creating distortions in the domestic market, protectionist policies drove many LDCs towards specialising in the wrong commodities or products, that is, products in which LDCs' true comparative advantage did not lie. By insulating their economies with tariffs and quotas, LDCs made it difficult for themselves to judge where their comparative advantage lay. The steep effective rates of protection also work against the declared policy interests of the governments. The Indian experience is an illustration of this point. After the first serious foreign exchange crisis in 1956–57, an elaborate bureaucratic system of QRs was installed by the Government of India. All requests to import were subject to administrative scrutiny; even the smallest items required a license for import. Furthermore, an import license was not available for goods which could be indigenously produced. This led to effective rates of protection which exceed 200 per cent on average. Imports of capital and intermediate goods were allowed, while those of consumer goods were banned. The consequence was that the effective rates of protection of – and hence incentives to invest in – the indigenous consumer goods industries was higher. Paradoxically the official policy during this period was to promote the heavy industries sector. Also, since the effective rates of exchange were much higher for importers than exporters, there was a bias against exports.[3] The Indian trade policy regime is considered appallingly inefficient, wasteful and corrupt.

Protection affects the marginal productivity of the factors of production, leading to their sub-optimal allocation. Both of these entailed severe welfare losses. Protectionist policies were also frequently justified on the basis of the existence of distortions in the domestic markets. But protection is not the optimal instrument to deal with these. By applying the general principles of trade policy, one can see that subsidies and taxation do a far superior job. Building on the work of Meade, Haberler and Viner, Bhagwati and Ramaswami published their seminal work rigorously establishing that most arguments for protection based on the need to correct distortions in the working of the domestic price mechanism were, in reality, arguments for domestic tax-cum-subsidies and not for protection.[4] If anything, protection could make the existing malaise worse.

The exports of the LDCs, particularly from the NICs, are of increasing importance in world trade. Therefore high barriers and illiberal trade regimes in the LDCs are a source of irritation in many industrial countries. In addition, the developing countries realised a trifle too late that by not reciprocating and passively accepting the 'special and differential' status they had struck a 'Faustian bargain'.[5] In exchange for preferences, which brought them limited and uncertain gains, they have given up a voice in reciprocal trade negotiations. The protectionist lobby in the industrial countries accuse them of unfair trade. Thus viewed, an illiberal trade regime has baneful ramifications both on domestic and international fronts. Countertrade has been popular with a large number of developing countries. Its volume has, however, stagnated since 1984, and declined since 1987.

The two exhaustive studies of the trade regimes of LDCs, that is, the ones commissioned by the National Bureau of Economic Research (NBER)[6] and the Organisation for Economic Co-operation and Development (OECD),[7] which provided an empirical validation of the theoretical case against protection, also gave estimates of protective structure for several developing countries. The NBER studies cover Argentina, Turkey, Israel, the Philippines and Ghana, while the OECD studies gave estimates for Brazil, India, Pakistan, the Philippines and Mexico. These studies gave tariff estimates as well as the effective protection rates. The synthesis volumes indicated that the average levels of tariff imposed by LDCs for manufactures are extremely high. By contrast, most industrial economies used substantially lower tariffs in the course of their economic development. This contrast is sustained by effective protection rates as well.

The labour-intensive sectors in LDCs tend to be protected more heavily than the capital-intensive ones. The effect of this structure of protection is to retard LDCs exports of labour-intensive goods to other LDCs more than those to the industrial countries. Therefore, the future prospects of LDCs' trade would be influenced not only by the policies of the industrial countries but also by the trade liberalisation measures taken by LDCs, in particular the more industrially advanced ones among them.

A sample survey of developing countries based on the UNCTAD data was done[8] to see the level of tariffs and their *ad valorem* incidence on imports. The results are tabulated on p. 48. For a sample of 42 developing countries, for which the simple average tariffs were computed, the *ad valorem* incidence of tariff was of the order of 12 per cent, while the average tariffs were at the level of 32 per cent.

Another sample survey of 35 LDCs done by the International Monetary Fund showed that, between 1978 and 1983, little overall change occurred in the restrictiveness of their exchange and trade systems.[9] Only a small number of LDCs relied on tariff protection; the majority used a combination of tariffs and

Table 3.1 UNWEIGHTED AVERAGE TARIFF RATES AND
THEIR *AD VALOREM* INCIDENCE ON IMPORTS IN
SELECTED LDCs

(In Percent)

Country	Year	Unweighted average tariffs	*Ad valorem* incidence of tariffs
Argentina	1977	27.0	8.2
Bahamas	1978	30.1	2.9
Bangladesh	1973	76.0	11.1
Benin	1977	30.9[a]	19.7[d]
Brazil	1978	40.3	8.8
Burkina Faso	1979	59.6[a]	25.8[a]
Burundi	1976	41.7[b]	12.6[b]
Chile	1978	22.6	10.1
Colombia	1977	28.0	12.3
Ecuador	1977	31.7	22.2
Egypt	1977	40.6	27.9
Gabon	1976	33.0[c]	14.6[c]
Ghana	1979	39.5	15.0
India	1976	72.0	28.8
Indonesia	1976	29.4	7.9
Iran	1977	22.3	11.4
Jamaica	1976	16.4	3.9
Korea, Rep. of	1978	29.9	8.8
Liberia	1979	26.0	13.9
Malawi	1977	11.0	7.8
Malaysia	1976	15.3	7.3
Mali	1979	31.4[a]	4.8[a]
Mexico	1977	22.3	7.2
Morocco	1978	30.7	8.7
Niger	1977	18.2[a]	10.7[a]
Nigeria	1977	26.7	14.7
Pakistan	1978	74.0	24.8
Panama	1979	14.1	3.7
Peru	1977	40.1	7.9
Philippines	1976	44.2	12.7
Rwanda	1975	27.8[d]	17.6[d]
Senegal	1979	46.4[a]	5.2[a]
Sierra Leone	1979	26.6	17.3
Singapore	1976	5.6	1.2
Somalia	1977	35.1[e]	22.9[e]

Sri Lanka	1976	38.8	9.7
Surinam	1976	24.5	16.3
Thailand	1976	29.4	12.4
Togo	1979	14.2	6.9
Tunisia	1977	18.2	8.0
Venezuela	1977	41.9	4.7
Zaire	1979	6.5	3.1
Average		31.9	11.9

a. Cumulative rate for customs and fiscal duty.
b. Cumulative rate (import duty 2.0 per cent and revenue import tax 39.7 per cent).
c. Cumulative rate (customs duty 11.0 per cent and fiscal duty 23.0 per cent).
d. Cumulative rate (customs duty 6.8 per cent and revenue duty 21.0 per cent).
e. Cumulative rate (customs duty 4.7 per cent and fiscal duty 30.4 per cent).

SOURCE   Tymowski (1987).

non-tariff measures. The available information confirmed that LDCs maintained a high average statutory level of tariffs, and that quantitative import restrictions were often used in conjunction with industrial licensing policies. Some sectors faced prohibitive statutory tariffs but import licenses were granted with substantial exception from tariffs in accordance with established sectoral objectives. This eventually exacerbated allocative distortions, and encouraged rent-seeking tendencies.

Protection was not always on infant industry grounds. In some sectors, several LDCs had a comparative advantage without the need to rely on protection. The textiles and clothing sector, for example, was found to have tariff levels of 10 to 50+ per cent in a sample of 21 LDCs.[10] These tariffs could hardly be justified. The NBER and OECD studies have noted a phased pattern in trade policy among the sample LDCs chosen by them. Their descriptions of various phases are lengthy and intricate; however, a succinct summary of the various policy stages can be made, as follows:

Phase I: Significant and frequent employment of QRs in a rather 'crude' and 'unsophisticated' fashion.

Phase II: QRs still reign, but the control mechanism be-
              comes complex and differentiated. Even when
              there are export subsidies, the effective exchange
              rate on exports is always lower than that on
              imports, which are highly protected.

Phase III: Tidying up operations are introduced. They may
              take the form of a devaluation-cum-liberalisation
              package. The tariff structure is rationalised.

Phase IV: This is a successful culmination of Phase III libera-
              lisation efforts. Incentives are made uniform.
              Inter alia, the effective exchange rate on exports is
              equated to that on imports.

Phase V: Full convertibility of the current account is at-
              tained. QRs are no longer used for balance of
              payments purposes. The flexible exchange rate is
              kept in equilibrium. Monetary and fiscal policies
              are employed as instruments to achieve payment
              balance instead of relying on exchange and import
              controls.

Phases I and III appear to be transitional phases, but the system
could rest on any one of the remaining three phases. Phases I
and II fall in inward-looking policy regimes, in contrast to
phases IV and V, which come under the outward-looking or
exporient-oriented policy regimes.

Recently there has been a growing recognition that economic
growth can be stepped up by pursuing less protective trade
policies. The intellectual hold of the legitimacy of protectionist
ideas weakened during the mid-1960s and early 1970s. It was
partly inspired by the astounding performance of the East Asian
NICs, and partly by the lethargic long-term performance of
countries like Argentina, Egypt and India which are at the
opposite extreme of the policy spectrum from the East Asians.
LDCs, therefore, have become relatively more disposed to
giving up illiberal trade regimes and the self-sufficiency-
oriented approach to economic growth. The liberalisation
measures taken lately by LDCs have varied, depending on the
prevailing balance of payments pressures and the extent of
distortions. In some cases the wisdom to liberalise trade was
home grown, in others these strategies were a part of the Fund
or World Bank-sponsored structured adjustment programmes.

In all cases applying appropriate exchange rate policies was a critical element in the corrective policy package.

Earlier in this section it has been noted that the two primal forces which drove LDCs towards restrictive trade regimes were related to the balance of payments imbalance and the protection of infant industries. The belief that tariffs or quantitative restrictions (QRs) can improve a country's current account was correct during the halcyon days of the Bretton Woods system, when exchange rates were fixed. We now live in a floating exchange rate world, and so the above belief is no longer valid. Exchange rate movements can be used to shift demand from imported goods to domestically produced ones.

The classic infant-industry argument for temporary protection has two main supports. First, it can be based on financial market imperfections. In the LDCs the financial markets may not be deep enough to provide capital to finance initial losses for an industry which would eventually become profitable and competitive. In such a case the best policy instrument is not tariffs or QRs, but improvement of the capital market, especially removing imperfections resulting from specific government policies. Second, protection can also rest on the premise of the existence of external economies of a dynamic kind applied to an industrial sector. The protected sector can be assumed to create a favourable environment for new kinds of industrial activities. This deserves to be treated with some scepticism because protection of one industry is always at the expense of others.[11]

4 THE GENERALISED SYSTEM OF PREFERENCES AND THE OTHER PREFERENTIAL TRADING AGREEMENTS

The earliest preferential trading agreements between the developing and the industrialised countries began as extensions of the former colonial, semi-colonial and strategic-political relations. For instance, the United States granted special preferences to exports from the Philippines in 1900. The European Economic Community, after the initiatives taken by France, made a preferential agreement with the Associated African Countries. Although the agreement was expanded under the Yaondé

Convention (1963), the basic ideas existed in the Treaty of Rome (1958). Under the Lomé Convention of 1975, 45 African, Caribbean and Pacific (ACP) countries were given special treatment for their exports to the European Economic Community. With the objective of fostering economic stability, the European Economic Community initiated preferential trade agreements with Greece in 1962 and Turkey in 1964. These agreements were aimed eventually to lead to full accession. Morocco and Tunisia received duty-free access for their industrial exports to the Community in 1969. Under the Caribbean Basin Economic Recovery Act of 1983, the United States provided preferential tariff treatment to most of the countries in the Caribbean Basin. As of today, virtually all the developing countries enjoy some sort of special access to the markets of the industrial countries. The most comprehensive preferential trade agreement, however, is the Generalised System of Preferences. Its genesis is set forth in the following paragraph.

At the time of UNCTAD I in 1964, Raul Prebisch prepared a study which focused international attention on the idea that preferential tariff rates in the markets of the industrialised countries could provide impetus to trade and growth in the LDCs. The underlying philosophy was that treating the developing and the industrialised countries on a par in the international trade arena would be unfair because equal treatment of unequals is inherently unequal, and would perpetuate and preserve inequality. The preferential tariff rates may be interpreted as a form of the infant-industry argument. Besides, the preferential arrangements can stimulate local production and help diversify the developing economy. Prebisch's study proposed the creation of a system of generalised non-reciprocal preferences, under which the industrial economies would lower the customs duties on goods imported from LDCs. The system was introduced at the UNCTAD II meeting in 1968. In 1971 the Contracting Parties approved a waiver from the MFN provisions of Article I in order to allow the industrial market economies to grant preferential tariff treatment to LDCs for a period of ten years. A change in the status of the Generalised System of Preferences (GSP) *vis-à-vis* the GATT framework was subsequently introduced by the Contracting Parties during the Tokyo Round in 1979. The 'Enabling Clause' provision of the Tokyo Round allowed developed countries to accord differential and more favourable treatment to LDCs without according such treatment to other Contracting Parties, which in effect made discrimination acceptable. A further GATT waiver was, therefore, not needed in order to continue the GSP after 1981.

The first countries to translate the preferential access into practice were those of the EEC, Japan and Norway in 1971, followed by Denmark, Finland, New Zealand, Sweden, Switzerland and Austria in 1972. Canada adopted the GSP in 1974 and the United States in 1976. Under the terms of most GSP agreements, preferential access can be extended to manufacturers and semi-manufacturers. A few agricultural commodities were also added during the Tokyo Round of MTNs. However, specific exclusions are made of textiles and clothing, leather products and steel. These are the products in which many LDCs have comparative advantage and have, therefore, specialised. In addition, most schemes subject the preferences to a variety of restrictions. For instance, in the EEC countries ceilings are applied to GSP commodities, effectively converting the GSP into a system of 'tariff-quotas'. Besides, the rules of origin and the rules of consignment further restrict the impact of GSP.[12] Since the GSP scheme was seen as disguised aid, it was tightly controlled by the donors in terms of beneficiaries and products.

Have the GSP and other similar programmes produced significant welfare gains? A debate has raged around this question for a while. The consensus is that inasmuch as the GSP was conceived as an unrequited transfer, it has generated few net benefits – that is not to deny that there have been some significant gains for a small number of LDCs.

Several empirical studies have delved into the trade and development effects of the major preferential trading schemes. The American trade preference scheme for the Philippines was intended to stimulate local processing of raw materials. Badgett examined the performance of the scheme for the export of hard fibre, abaca, copra and raw sugar. For each of these products, time-series analysis was used to test the power of the preferential margins in explaining the ratio of processed to unprocessed exports to the United States, the rest of the world and total exports by the Philippines. Regression results indicated that tariff preferences resulted in a shift in the Philippines export of processed products away from the rest of the world and towards the United States. However, there was neither a change in the composition of the Philippines' exports, nor an increase in the total exports. The exporters gained only from the transfer of tariff revenue from the United States.[13] The empirical evaluations of the American trade preferences to the Caribbean Basin countries are limited to partial equilibrium studies. Sawyer and Sprinkle (1984) estimated that as a result of the preferences the imports of 20 top product categories would rise by $97 million, based on 1980 trade data, and that imports in all other product categories would rise by only $12 million. In all, the preference arrangement was expected to increase American imports from the Caribbean region by only 1 per cent. Trade creation accounted for $102 million in increased imports and the remaining $7 million was the result of trade diversion.[14] Another study indicated that exports from these developing countries to the United States would increase between $37 and $81 million, depending on elasticity assumptions. The welfare gain by the beneficiary countries was estimated to be between $15 and $24 million, which was only 6 per cent of aid in the form of direct US grants to the Caribbean countries.[15] Pelzman and Schoepfle (1986) computed the trade effects by comparing actual exports of the Caribbean basin to the United States to projections in the absence of preferences. The results were identical to those arrived at by the other two studies. They estimated a gross trade creation effect of $90 million in 1984, and an additional $12 million in 1985. The increase in trade was about 20 per cent in the articles covered by the preference scheme, but only 1.5 per cent of the total exports of the Caribbean basin countries to the United States.[16]

The trade preference arrangement between the European Economic Community and the Associated African Countries (AAC) was examined by Ouattara (1973) who found that in the pre-union period (1953–58), France imported 38 per cent of the AAC exports, and the rest of the members of the Community imported 34 per cent. Between 1959 and 1964 the Community's share (excluding France) remained constant, but that of France fell marginally. The trade pattern changed markedly between 1964 and 1968, when the French share declined to 32 per cent and that of the remaining Community countries rose to 38 per cent. Over the entire period, however, the Community's share declined from 72 to 69 per cent, indicating little evidence of trade creation.[17] The Community offered the most generous preferential treatment to the African, Caribbean and Pacific (CAP) countries. But these developing countries were poor exporters and have stayed so. Their exports are concentrated in a narrow range of primary commodities. They have few exportables in the manufacturing sector, and supply only 1 per cent of manufactured imports by the EEC from developing countries. The CAP countries have lost their share of the community market over the years, and have fared worse than other non-oil producing developing countries. The preferential agreement had little success in stimulating trade or industrialisation in the CAP countries.

Likewise, a few cost-benefit analyses of the GSP have been made. According to an OECD study,[18] in 1980, out of total dutiable imports of $179 billion entering the OECD countries from the GSP beneficiaries, $25.4 billion, or 14.0 per cent, were accorded GSP treatment. These GSP imports constituted about 8.0 per cent of the total imports from the beneficiaries when one includes other imports from these countries which do not bear import duties. Likewise, in 1981 the United States imported $120.3 billion worth from LDCs. From the GSP beneficiaries, the total imports were $68.5 billion, and of this only a meagre $8.4 billion, or 12.3 per cent, entered duty free.

For the exports of the non-oil LDCs, the United States is the largest market, exceeding the EEC or Japan. According to the 1985 statistics, the value (fob) of LDCs' exports to the USA stood at $111.9 billion, and those to the EEC and Japan were $90.4 billion and $60.5 billion, respectively. The implementation of GSP in the United States illustrates the limitations of the system. As noted, import sensitive items, which include textiles, apparel, footwear, certain kinds of steel and electronic articles, are not eligible for the GSP. Even with respect to eligible products, the American scheme provides uncertain benefits. Under the 'competitive need' tests mandated by US law, a beneficiary LDC loses GSP privileges for a particular product if its exports to the US exceed 50 per cent of the value of total United States imports of that product. Further, as noted, in certain product lines, some LDCs were later removed from the US GSP beneficiary list in response to petitions filed by the American producers or trade unions.

A study assessing the trade effects of the American GSP concluded that gross trade creation amounted to $1 billion and trade diversion to $0.4 billion.[19] The total $1.4 billion represented 3.0 per cent of US imports from the GSP beneficiaries in 1979. A larger share of benefits for LDCs are likely to come from the reduction in the US protection rather than from the market preferences under the GSP. If a similar study of the EEC is undertaken, it is likely that it would also show that the GSP rendered only limited benefits to LDCs.[20] For the OECD as a whole, the proportion of imports from GSP beneficiaries in 1980 was only 8.0 per cent, against 13.0 per cent for the United States. Besides, although the details of the schemes differ, the European Community's and the Japanese schemes are more restrictive because they include country quotas, ceilings and maximum amount limits imposed on the beneficiary LDCs.[21]

There is no semblance of evenness in the distribution of GSP benefits. A large part of imports was concentrated in a small number of products and a small number of LDCs, which already had a significant market share in those products. A large part of the benefits has been reaped by only four beneficiaries, namely, Hong Kong, Korea (Republic of), Taiwan and Brazil. All four are NICs. Under the various US GSP schemes, 140 LDCs are on the list as eligible beneficiaries, but almost half the benefits go to Hong Kong, Taiwan and Korea (Republic of). Only ten LDCs supply 80 per cent of all GSP imports, and the list of countries has remained by and large the same in 1986 as was in 1980.[22]

The direct trade benefits to LDCs have been estimated as follows: taking an aggregated view, $6 536 million, or 2.3 per cent, of imports by the GSP donor countries from the preference receiving LDCs can be attributed to the GSP.[23] A great deal of the increase in imports has been the result of trade diversion of the other exporters; in this case they were the industrialised countries themselves. According to a recent estimate, in gross terms, the benefits available under the schemes of the EEC ($2.4 billion) and the United States ($2.3 billion) were in each case several times larger than the benefits under the scheme of the next largest donor (Japan $0.74 billion), and together these two schemes are estimated to have accounted for over 70.0 per cent of the direct trade effects of the combined schemes.[24]

Tariffs in the industrial countries are higher on the exports of manufactured products from LDCs; they are particularly high on many of the key GSP products. This seems to run counter to one of the main propositions of the GSP, namely to increase the industrialisation in LDCs. Thus, in key manufactured exports GSP provides limited relief from the high tariff rates. Moreover, limitations like the MFA, and other NTBs, ensure that even these reliefs are not fully exploited by the exporting LDCs. Only about one-fourth of the dutiable products from beneficiary LDCs are able to benefit from preferential entry. The possibility of realising full gains from the GSP depends to a large extent on the removal of the NTBs. Many of these barriers are of long-standing and bitterly disputed, and cannot be eschewed in the short-term.

In the first blush, the creation of preferential trading agreements and the GSP was acclaimed as a valuable, meaningful and necessary compromise of the MFN principle. But the restrictive nature of many agreements subsequently stimulated widespread disaffection among the LDCs. They have expressed concern about the unilateral and non-binding character of the GSP concessions. In particular, they objected to the possibility of arbitrary withdrawals. The fact that GSP concessions are not binding like the MFN concessions, means that they can be altered or even revoked at short notice.[25]

In all the preferential trade agreements, including the GSP, the extent of preferences is limited by a variety of mechanisms. For example, the Community does not grant tariff preferences on metals and most agricultural products. As noted, the textile and clothing quotas are determined by the Multifibre Arrangement. The Economic Community also places quantitative limits on imports eligible for duty-free treatment. Furthermore, quotas on sensitive products are administered at the member-country level. Individual beneficiary developing countries have further limits. Likewise, the United States excludes watches, import-sensitive electronic items, several steel varieties, footwear and import–sensitive glass products from its trade preference schemes. Many of these products are of special interest to the developing countries, particularly the newly industrialising countries. As noted, the United States has an interesting law which stipulates that developing countries whose exports exceed 50 per cent of the total import in a product category in a single calendar year, will be subject to the MFN rate in that product category in the following year. Like the United States and the EEC, Japan has a list of products excluded from the GSP. Also, quantitative limits are imposed using a system similar to that maintained by the Community.[26] The ultimate effect of the various lists of exclusions is severe limits on the GSP programmes of the industrialised countries. Besides, the United States and the Community have made it obvious that they believe in the concept of graduation and from time to time the beneficiaries would be graduated to the MFN rates. In 1981 both withdrew GSP concessions from several NICs, on the grounds that they were no longer in need of preferential treatment. Such withdrawals affect the security of LDCs' access to the industrial countries' markets; in effect it increases the risk in investing in export industries.

Another practice undermining the benefits of the GSP is the insistence on conditionality. Some countries, like the United States, have recently expected reciprocal action on the part of the GSP beneficiary. This clearly violates the original concensus regarding GSP benefits. The basic precept was that they were not to be based on reciprocity of concessions by the beneficiary LDCs. The GSP loses its meaning if reciprocity is applied to it. Besides, Article XXXVI of the GATT charter forbids any demand for reciprocal concessions from the LDCs.[27] The non-discriminatory feature of the GSP has been under assault. Unilaterally repealing the GSP in certain markets has seriously eroded its value and utility. There is some evidence that the withdrawal of GSP benefits from the better off LDCs has proved to be of little benefit to the trade of the poorer LDCs. Excluding selected LDCs, because they are the most successful and least cost exporters, reflects the victory of protectionist interests in the importing countries.

5   THE STATE OF TRADE POLICIES IN THE 1980s

During the postwar period seven rounds of multilateral trade negotiations took place, which succeeded in substantial tariff reductions, mainly on manufactured goods. The eighth round is presently underway. The recommendations of the last round, namely the Tokyo Round (1973–79), were implemented by the end of 1987, taking the average tariff level in the major OECD countries down to 6.0 to 7.0 per cent. The average tariff level in

1947 was 40.0 per cent. In addition, tariff barriers have been eliminated for trade in industrial goods within and between the two major trading blocs, namely, the European Economic Community (EEC) and the European Free Trade Area (EFTA).

The other side of the coin is that the tariffs vary among commodities and tend to be higher on the products of interest to developing countries (see Table 3.1). They also continue to escalate from a lower to higher level as the degree of processing and fabrication rises, thus discriminating against the export of processed goods from LDCs.

Trade in agriculture is wellnigh out of the ambit of the General Agreement on Tariff and Trade (GATT). During various rounds of the multilateral trade negotiations (MTNs) several products of primary export interest to LDCs were not paid enough attention; the reasons for this have already been set forth. Agricultural products were largely kept out of the negotiations. Temperate agricultural products were hardly touched, but tropical ones did benefit in a limited way. Also, manufactured products of interest to LDCs have had less than average tariff reductions in the MTNs. Tariffs have also persisted against other primary exports from LDCs.

The average tariffs before and after implementation of the Tokyo Round in the industrial countries has been estimated as follows on p. 60:

Table 3.2 PRE- AND POST-TOKYO ROUND TARIFF
STRUCTURES

(In per cent)

Importer	Tariff on total imports of finished and semi-finished manufactures		Tariffs on imports from LDCs of finished and semi-finished manufactures	
	Pre-Tokyo	Post-Tokyo	Pre-Tokyo	Post-Tokyo
1. EEC				
Weighted	8.3	6.0	8.9	6.7
Simple	9.4	6.6	8.5	5.8
2. Japan				
Weighted	10.0	5.4	10.0	6.8
Simple	10.8	6.4	11.0	6.7
3. USA				
Weighted	7.0	4.9	11.0	8.7
Simple	11.6	6.6	12.0	6.7

SOURCE   GATT, *The Tokyo Round of Multilateral Trade Negotiations*,
Vol. 2, Supplementary Report, Geneva, 1980, p. 37.

Plus Ça Change, Plus C'est la Même Chose

As the tariff barriers went down, another source of distortion to
international trade became more visible. The lowering of tariffs
was like the draining of a swamp, the lower water level revealed
all the snags and stumps of non-tariff barriers (NTBs). Since the
early 1970s the NTBs have grown at an alarming rate, and the
situation threatens to get out of hand. The GATT code deals
with tariff barriers and forbids non-tariff barriers (NTBs); they
are only allowed under special circumstances. There has also
been a rise in 'process protectionism' – the use of semi-judicial
mechanisms to discourage imports. The other new barriers are
of the kind that attempt to restrict free trade and convert it into
'managed' trade, encourage bilateral trading arrangements in
place of multilateral trade, and impose voluntary export restraints (VERs) and orderly marketing arrangements (OMAs) on
trading partners. The latter two are euphemisms for flagrant

and undisguised mercantilistic practices. All these divert trade, create artificial scarcity rents and weaken GATT discipline.

Unlike tariffs, which operate openly and through the price mechanism, non-tariff barriers are often of a covert nature, if not opaque. It is, therefore, difficult to estimate the impact of these measures or at times even discover their existence. Little information is available on the actual impact of known NTBs on various LDCs and on the volume of trade in various product lines. One can only hazard a guestimate. In addition, they are known to introduce greater rigidities into the international trading system and are applied on a discriminatory basis.

The successful exporters among LDCs have felt constrained by the frequent use of the safeguard clause by the industrialised countries.[28] For example, the provisions of Article XIX were used by the United States since 1986 to protect more than 30 industries, ranging from integrated steel to manufactures of nuts and bolts. As seen in Table 3.3 the EEC has used it far more. The language of Article XIX is oblique and lends itself to abuse. It has, in fact, become the Achilles heel of multilateral trade negotiations and will continue to be so for years to come. It is unfortunate because, due to technological and other developments, the international comparative advantage is changing faster than before, yet misuse of Article XIX, or bypassing it, makes it difficult to take advantage of these developments in the realm of international trade. The industrial countries often bypass the safeguard clause and take discriminatory measures which Article XIX does not permit.

Instead of toeing the line of Article XIX, the instruments used by the industrialised countries are, as noted, the orderly-marketing arrangements and the voluntary export restraints. They are euphemistically referred to as the 'grey area' measures and have been in circulation since the mid-1970s. These measures are fundamentally at variance with the principle of non-discrimination as expressed in Articles I and VIII, and are a clear abrogation of the multilaterialism of international trade. They are easy to apply and provide a short cut to protection against imports because no legislative action is needed.[29] The use of 'grey area' measures is expanding fast. At last count, in September 1987, GATT officials spotted 135 'grey area' measures, a rise from 93 in September 1986. There are several less formal measures in vogue as well, the terminology about which

Table 3.3 EXPORT RESTRAINT ARRANGEMENTS IN FORCE IN SEPTEMBER 1986

	Steel	Machine tools	Transport equipment	Electronic products	Footwear	Textiles	Agricultural products	Other	Total
EEC									
Number	14[a]	2	9	5	1	3	15	4	53
Price controls	12	1	–	3	–	–	–	–	16
Quality restrictions	–	–	9	2	–	2	15	–	28
Other	2	1	–	–	1	1	–	4	9
United States									
Number	25	1	1	1	–	4	–	–	32
Price controls	–	1	–	1	–	–	–	–	2
Quality restrictions	24	–	1	–	–	4	–	–	29
Other	1	–	–	–	–	–	–	–	1
Other									
Number	–	–	3	–	3	4	–	1	11
Price controls	–	–	–	–	–	–	–	–	–
Quality restrictions	–	–	3	–	2	3	–	–	8
Other	–	–	–	–	1	1	–	–	3
Total									
Number	39	3	13	6	4	11	15	5	96
Price controls	12	2	–	4	–	–	–	–	18
Quality restrictions	24	–	13	2	2	9	15	–	65
Other	3	1	–	–	2	3	–	4	12

SOURCE GATT, *Developments in the Trade System. April–September 1986*, Geneva, Appendix V(a), pp. 75–82.

is somewhat fluid. They are referred to as export forecasts, consultation arrangements, industry-to-industry arrangements, prudent marketing arrangements, and the like. These are export monitoring arrangements without a firm commitment to a quota or market share. All of these are para-legal measures framed outside the GATT and are restrictive in nature.

A large proportion of trade between industrial market economies takes place without tariffs but, as I have stated, the labour-intensive goods and manufactures in which LDCs have a comparative advantage, are subject to the highest tariffs. Even after the Tokyo Round this situation has not been ameliorated.[30] In addition, LDCs have to clear non-tariff barriers, which are often not binding, as well as hard-core non-tariff barriers in the form of quantitative restrictions (QRs). The protectionistic effects of the restrictive measures – measured in terms of the level of prevented imports – are particularly large because the demand for the kinds of exports named above has a relatively low income elasticity and high price elasticity. The majority of restrictive measures are industry or sector specific, and are designed to increase the level of output and employment in a particular industry or sector.

In the period from, say, 1949 – the first, Geneva Round of multilateral trade negotiations – to about 1963, the launching of the Kennedy Round, trade policy negotiations were largely centred on tariffs. Even the Kennedy Round (1964–67) neglected the non-tariff trade distortions. In fact, its neglect of such distortions was as disappointing as its tariff-reducing accomplishments were encouraging. The multilateral negotiations have now shifted to the non-tariff barriers (NTBs) and the operation of 'managed' trade arrangements, like the multifibre arrangement (MFA), and the deployment of various discretionary, discriminatory techniques of intervention. These techniques include anti-dumping and countervailing duties, the so-called 'safeguard' action, as well as measures like investment grants and low-interest loans to export or import-substituting sectors, wage subsidies in selected manufacturing industries, and other forms of export subsidies. At the time of the Kennedy Round it was generally felt that since the GATT deals with many of these policies only in a cursory manner, both a code of behaviour and procedures for enforcing it were needed. The NTBs, accordingly, were addressed in the Tokyo Round (1973–79), and while some progress was made in devising the code to restrain some forms of NTBs, progress in enforcement of the code was tardy. The problem still persists and continues to impede multilateral trade flows. Little wonder that NTBs are high on the agenda of the current Uruguay Round (1986–90). The growing importance of NTBs is but one manifestation of the growing economic interdependence of nations. Increasingly national governments have become disposed to intervene in their domestic economies, and their interventions are increasingly likely to affect the economic interests of citizens of other countries.

The three most important sets of NTBs presently affecting LDC exports are in textiles and apparel, agriculture and steel. However, they are not limited to these products and are wide-ranging. One is struck by the variety of products which are subject to NTBs. For example, 97.8 per cent of four digit CCCN (Customs Co-operative Council Nomenclature) product groups face a prohibition somewhere in the world, often in more than one country. The UNCTAD secretariat conducted a comprehensive study of NTBs in operation in the developing and industrialised countries. It estimated that 23.2 per cent of the import categories of the industrialised countries are currently subject to volume controls, while 7.5 per cent are subject to some form of non-tariff price restrictions, such as variable import levies or anti-dumping levies.[31] An OECD study suggests that between 1963 and 1983 the number of NTBs quadrupled and that there was an increase in the proportion of trade affected within protected sectors. For instance, in steel the proportion of trade affected by NTBs increased from 37.0 per cent to 73.0 per cent.[32] At the 1982 GATT ministerial session, a GATT list of some 600 NTBs was discussed.

The results of an empirical exercise show that if tariffs in the industrial countries are replaced by a mean-preserving equal-rate tariff on all products which are imported from the developing countries, the gains to the NICs would be worth $1.6 billion and those to other LDCs $1.9 billion.[33] This shows that some high tariffs that operate in the industrial countries on certain items of export interest to LDCs, like textiles and clothing, are significant deterrents. If all industrial countries were to remove NTBs on all agricultural imports, the gains to the developing countries would be substantial, because agricultural exports are of great importance to many of them. Estimates show that the gains are of the order of $5.3 billion to the NICs and $6.7 billion to other LDCs. If NTBs were removed from agricultural imports from the developing countries only, the gains would naturally be larger. They would be $7.0 billion for the NICs and $9.4 billion for the other LDCs.[34] But such action would contravene the GATT charter.

The LDCs use quantitative controls to a much greater extent than the industrial market economies. From a sample of 22 LDCs at different stages of economic growth, it was found that 70.5 per cent of import categories are subject to non-tariff price restrictions. There is another assessment of trade intervention measures applied by LDCs, based on statistical data supplied by 50 LDCs. This is in the form of frequency indices for product-specific measures and across-the-board measures such as foreign exchange restrictions for balance of payments purposes.[35] The results are summarised below:

Table 3.4 FREQUENCY MEASURES OF THE APPLICATION OF NTBs FROM A SAMPLE OF 50 LDCs (1985–86)

(In per cent)

	NTBs		Of which Quantitative Restrictions			
	All	Product specific	Total	Discretionary license	Quotas	Prohibitions
Simple average	57.6	26.9	34.8	28.6	2.6	4.8
Trade-Weighted average	40.2	27.0	23.5	17.7	0.9	5.5

NB   NTBs include volume and price-restraining measures as well as product-specific measures.

SOURCE   UNCTAD 1987. Gleaned from Annex, 36, p. A–37.

The unweighted frequency ratio of general measures is 57.6 per cent, while the ratio of product-specific NTBs is 26.9 per cent. The reason the trade-weighted average of general measure is markedly lower at 40.2 per cent is that NTB applications tend to be more frequent in smaller LDCs. Smaller countries have small trade volumes, and therefore lower trade-weighted indices are obtained. A marked characteristic of the frequency ratio for LDCs is that intervention is widespread across sectors. However, unlike the industrial economies, the NTBs are not strongly biased in favour of particular sectors. The upshot is that the *ad valorem* equivalent protection is significantly higher in LDCs than in the industrial market economies.

The most recent developments in this regard are that, during 1986–88, a clutch of relatively better off LDCs substantially liberalised their tariff policies. This resulted from both autonomous changes in the orientation of trade policies and external factors. The Republic of Korea, Nigeria and Taiwan reduced tariff rates on a large number of products. This apart, substantial tariff reductions were also implemented in Ghana, Indonesia, Morocco, Mali and Mauritius. As for the quantitative restrictions, an easing was observed in Argentina, Colombia, Morocco, the Republic of Korea, Indonesia, the Philippines, Taiwan, Tunisia, Turkey and Yugoslavia. Mexico and Morocco – which acceded to GATT in June 1987 – reduced contingency protection by relying more on tariffs as part of programmes aimed at rationalisation and liberalisation of their foreign trade regimes.[36] Contrary to these developments, certain LDCs were forced to retrogress; due to adverse balance-of-payments pressures they intensified their import restrictions.

6   TRADE IN SERVICES

Trade in services was neglected for a long while by the international community, and trade theory made no allusion to it, although in recent years it has come into prominence. This is because of progressive internationalisation of a number of service industries and their increasing contribution to externally-oriented growth and employment. Services have a tradition of protection both in developing and developed countries. The World Development Report 1987 lists several interesting examples: (1) Colombian imports can be insured only by Colombian companies; (2) India does not allow foreign insurance firms to operate and foreign banks can operate in a limited manner only; (3) foreign communications firms are barred in Belgium, Italy and the Netherlands; (4) foreign construction firms are restricted in Brazil, and they cannot construct and design oil-drilling platforms in the UK; (5) in Pakistan cinemas are required to devote 15 per cent of playing time to local films; (6) Italy requires the hiring of local actors and film crews to make commercials; and (7) Argentina, Mexico, Peru and Venezuela insist on having local accountants supervising foreign auditors. The office of the United States Trade Representatives has a long inventory of foreign trade barriers in services. It is, however, far from exhaustive. The upshot is that there are few countries, developed or developing, that allow foreigners to compete on an equal footing with the locals in the arena of trade in services.

The trade in services is less straightforward than that in goods, essentially because services can be provided in a variety of ways and encompass an externally heterogenous group of economic sub-sectors, with different production processes, customers, suppliers and market channels. In the goods trade, even if foreign competition decimates a segment of the economy, the resulting reallocation of resources could strengthen the whole economy. In the case of trade in services, more than just allocative efficiency is at stake. International trade in services may, indeed, bring about a better allocation of resources, but it influences other aspects of the overall performance of economies as well.[37] Unlike the trade in goods, trade in services does not come under the GATT framework. The statistical data on international trade in services are fragmentary and not sufficiently broken down. However, from the available data, it is not difficult to estimate that it has been growing at a brisk pace: the electronic revolution and information technology have helped its fast expansion. According to the United States Department of Commerce Statistics (1985), the total recorded world exports in services was $336 billion in 1983, compared to only $91 billion in 1971. For both years these amounts represent about a fifth of world merchandise exports. Be it noted that 'services' include investment income. In the industrialised countries, between 1976 and 1986, the growth of trade in services has been faster than the growth of trade in goods. During 1986 services accounted for half of all Britain's exports compared with 35.0 per cent in 1976. Britain's strength reflects its position as both a centre of finance and a leading international creditor. Austria, which had the second highest share of services in its exports,[38] owes its ranking to tourism. In the developing countries the average rate of growth of services output has been higher than that of GNP during the last 10 to 12 years. This contrasts with the trend in the 1960s, when the reverse was true. The industrial market economies dominate both imports and exports in the services sector.

Countries having the highest amount of trade in services reveal significant differences among themselves. Factor endowments play the same role in trade in services as they do in trade in goods. For the most part, the industrialised countries display comparative advantage in skill- and capital-intensive services like banking, insurance and passenger and freight transport. The comparative advantage of LDCs lies in labour-intensive services such as tourism and construction. The LDCs of the Caribbean, Latin American and the Mediterranean areas already have well developed tourism. India and Korea (Republic of) have been successfully exporting construction services. Several LDCs which have invested heavily in education, and therefore, have a highly trained labour force, may earn good returns on their investments in such areas as the export of computer software and R & D services. Of the two, the former is already an established part of the trade in services and is growing.[39] Apart from the natural factor endowments, economic history, geographical location, structure and the nature of exports and movements of migrant workers influence the trade balance in services. An example is shipping: given that LDCs own only about 10 per cent of the world fleet, whereas they export 60 per cent of the commodities transported by ships, this leads to a deficit on trade in shipping services. Another example is oil and bulk cargo carrying; again LDCs own only 16.0 per cent of the world fleet while their exports in this category are 90.0 per cent of the total. Little wonder that the major oil-exporters and dry cargo (for example, cereals, meat) exporters also have large deficits under this item.[40]

Sampson and Snape's categorisation of trade in services offers a clear conceptualisation.[41] They divided trade in services into four functional categories:

(1)   Transactions that occur without the international move-
      ment of either the factors producing services or the re-
      ceivers of the services. This includes insurance, banking,
      consulting and provision of technological information.
      These services are supplied through correspondence and
      other standard means of communication by productive
      factors located in the exporting country to the recipients in
      the importing country.
(2)   Transactions that take place as a consequence of the
      international movement of productive factors but not the
      receivers of the services. The provision of banking,
      transportation and construction services, which involves
      the movement of productive factors to the importing
      country, are illustrations of this category. This implies that
      for trade in certain types of services the functionaries need
      to be moved, or possibly full branches of business need to
      be established, into the importing country. Such services
      are known as 'temporarily-factor-relocation-requiring'
      services. For some services the factor relocation is not
      temporary.
(3)   Transactions that occur with the international movement
      of the receiver of the services but not the providers.
      Tourism and education fall into this category.
(4)   Transactions involving the movement of both the product-
      ive factors and the receivers of the services. An illustration
      of this is one country's ships or planes transporting goods
      and people from another country to a third country.

Following Sampson and Snape's classification, it is easy to see
that trade in services that fits in the first category is identical to
that in goods. Insofar as there are no barriers on the transmis-
sion of information by mail, telegraph and electronic means,
this trade can take place unimpeded. The second category of
trade, however, runs into problems, since the provision of
services usually involves direct investment in the consuming
country and/or the influx of foreign labour. Most countries
have definite policies in these matters, which include visa
requirements, investment regulations, restrictions on the ability
to repatriate earnings, and so on. Many LDCs wish to give
foreigners only limited control over their economic activity and
productive resources. Particular problems exist in banking and
insurance sectors because the presence of foreign firms here

would amount to interference in the monetary and fiscal policies of the importing LDCs. Ambivalence about the movement of foreign labour into their countries is common. Each country has its own immigration laws and the movements of foreign workers must comply with them, which makes the issue complex. Trade falling in the third category is not banned, but restrictions on foreign exchange spending on tourism and education are endemic.

The Newest Disputes

The United States pressed for the inclusion of trade in services in the GATT framework, and considered the Uruguay Round as the most ideal opportunity to do so. Most industrial countries joined the United States, while the key LDCs were opposed. The polarisation in this issue was not along North-South lines. Instead there was a formation of negotiating blocs of like-minded countries. A group of ten LDCs, known as the Group of Ten, vociferously led by Brazil and India, was opposed to the inclusion of services in the agenda of the Uruguay Round. Many of the smaller LDCs deserted this position and instead joined the major industrialised countries in the so-called Group of Forty-eight. The latter group was led by the United States, largely because this was the period when its merchandise trade registered unprecedented levels of deficits and a liberalisation of trade in services would have helped improve its current account.

The LDCs which were averse to the inclusion of services in the Uruguay Round contended that for a wide range of services they were in no position to compete with the industrialised countries, either in their own domestic markets or in world markets. They argued that liberalising trade in services could adversely affect the growth of their domestic services sectors, and in the long run could undermine their international competitive position in both goods and services. It would also reduce the value added derived from international trade and inhibit the growth of small- and medium-sized firms.[42]

Their opposition was also due to the fear of a trade-off between trade in goods and trade in services; in other words the industrialised countries would not open their markets to LDCs' goods without getting in return some service penetration in

LDC markets. Economically this apprehension was somewhat ill-founded because this argument presupposes a water-tight compartmentalisation of sectors–resources, goods, services – which is far from the reality. In all sectors services are a key input to production.

The contention of the developing countries was that if inclusion of services in the GATT or trade liberalisation in this sector is to be meaningful from the perspective of the LDCs, other initiatives need to be taken to assist them in overcoming obstacles to market entry. For instance, the labour-cost advantage of LDCs is frustrated by stringent immigration laws in most industrial economies. A liberal permit requirement is imperative for encouraging trade in services sectors where labour is an important factor in the 'services package'. This would augment trade in professional and other services. Second, earnings from tourism can benefit from selective measures like tax deductions for overseas business conventions. Several similar measures could be planned before trade in services is liberalised.

Admittedly, any negotiations to liberalise trade in services are bound to be difficult and time-consuming because grouping together many disparate activities for meaningful unified negotiations will pose several conceptual problems. Special problems would emerge in the fields of banking and insurance, which are intertwined with national monetary and fiscal affairs. It is also likely that the achievements may be so meagre that negotiations in these sectors will not be worthwhile. Similarly, the movement of workers and professionals is likely to come up against the immigration laws of importing countries, and may not make much progress.

4 The Erosion of the GATT Framework

1 THE FRAMEWORK

Inasmuch as free trade is in the interest of all countries, one wonders why a formal structure of co-operation is needed at all. Yet it was largely due to the GATT that the tariff walls came down, and now it is the principal line of defence against the new upsurge of protectionism. Again, it is the only international body which is concerned with control over and elimination of the non-tariff barriers which impede international trade and distort competition. The GATT is largely needed because the politics of free trade is much trickier than the economics. The GATT framework has, essentially, been devised for the market-oriented economic system, under which the difference between international and domestic prices would be the main determinant of international trade flows. Admittedly, it is an idealistic vision of the GATT, which, in reality, like any other international agreement, is a product of compromises. It has been inspired by the interwar experience of trade restrictions, bilateralism, uncertainty and the ultimate collapse of the international trading system. The GATT accord, therefore, is based on non-discrimination, reciprocity, transparency and openness in the trading system. It has emerged out of the negotiated general rules of behaviour for the Contracting Parties, with an objective to ensure stability and predictability in international trade. The emphasis is on the *negotiated*, that is, negotiated and agreed upon general rules, and specific mutually negotiated trade concessions.

The GATT is not a formal treaty but an executive agreement. It is an agreement on a number of basic principles or norms of behaviour which, if followed, would contribute to an orderly evolution of an international market economy. The GATT is neither a judicial system, nor an enforcement body. Yet, one of its most important functions is to provide mechanisms for conciliation and settlement of disputes between the Contracting

Parties on trade related issues. The GATT is more than a set of trade regulations. It is a belief in and commitment to the liberalisation of world trade by the member sovereign states. It is also described as a system of 'balanced rights and obligations'

A code of conduct is imperative because international trade entails specialisation, which has a high cost in terms of time and resources. No country would want to specialise for a world market if it knew that its sources of imports or its markets for exports could be arbitrarily cut off at any time. If this were to be so, a retrograde motion towards autarky would set in.

2   GATT VIS-À-VIS THE INTERNATIONAL ECONOMY

The basic tenet of the GATT is enshrined in its first Article, which relates to the most-favoured-nation (MFN) principle. It is the key Article and is based on the efficiency approach to world trade. It states, 'With respect to customs duties and charges of any kind imposed on or in connection with importation or exportation . . . any advantage, favour, privilege or immunity granted by any Contracting Party to any product originating in or destined for any other country shall be accorded immediately and unconditionally to the like product originating in or destined for the territories of all other Contracting Parties'. However, neither the letter nor the spirit of GATT is always adhered to in the actual conduct of international trade. The dispute solving mechanism of the GATT is slow and has no teeth. It is the toothless policeman of international trade.[1] It has no sanctioning powers and its secretariat is primarily concerned with analytical, advisory and administrative functions.[2] The Contracting Parties can ask for a dispute panel to be appointed to report on a breach of the rules by another Contracting Party. But any recommendations are put into effect only if the country is willing to do so. The EEC twice side-stepped recommendations of the panel on agricultural trade with America, while the United States ignored the GATT decision against it once.

As expounded in Chapter 3, the first five rounds of the MTN were devoted to slashing and binding of tariff rates. During the Kennedy Round (1963–67) tariff negotiations again were at centre stage, though an attempt was made to address the NTBs. Unlike its predecessors, the Tokyo Round (1973–79) focused on the NTBs.

A smoothly functioning GATT would favourably influence the rhythm of the international economy. It has been observed that when the international economy – and, therefore, the markets – expand the trade of the LDCs grows too. During the buoyant periods of the international economy, the export growth rates of LDCs have averaged around 12.0 per cent a year under export-oriented regimes, assuming that domestic policies were appropriate. However, when the rhythm of the international economy was slow and, therefore, less favourable, the export growth rate of the same set of LDCs, under the same domestic policy regimes, averaged 5.0 to 7.0 per cent.[3] Thus, the growth rate of the international economy and the expansion of markets are of vital importance for LDCs trying to expand their trade and integrate into the international economy, and so is the GATT and its role.

3   THE SETTING IN OF EROSION

The GATT, to begin with, never had the resources or influence of its sister economic institutions in the field of finance and development, namely, the Bretton Woods Institutions. At the time of its inception, it was referred to as a 'slender reed' on which to base the progress towards a free, multilateral trading regime. In recent years, its charter has increasingly been ignored by the Contracting Parties, in particular by the large industrial economies. In cases of dispute, they have chosen increasingly to fight out their trade battles bilaterally, rather than go through GATT's slow-moving dispute procedures. During the two postwar decades the GATT provided an effective framework of negotiating trade liberalisation and upholding the liberal trading order. But there has been a progressive loss of confidence in its ability to enforce fair-trade rules. There has been an incessant erosion in its status. There are contrary trends in international trade, threatening to reverse the whole postwar process of trade liberalisation. The GATT is often referred to as 'in disarray' and 'moribund'. The erosion is manifested in a variety of features:

(1)   a repeated neglect of the unconditional MFN principle, let it be recalled, that non-discrimination is the bedrock principle of the GATT. Non-discrimination was never universally accepted, but attitudes and policies have without hinderance evolved further in the opposite direction;

(2)   the utilisation of concepts like 'market disruption' and 'conditional MFN' to provide justification for discriminatory measures;

(3)   the recent decline of the relevance of tariffs as an instrument of trade policy;

(4)   an increased resort to NTBs;

(5)   the proliferation of mechanisms for the management of the quantity, prices and often the sources of imports;

(6)   the application of discriminatory trade measures against LDCs, and frequent abuse of the safeguard clause;

(7)   a general emphasis on bilateral trade flows and a slow drift away from multilateralism.[4]

The fundamental norms, like non-discrimination and the use of tariffs as the only instrument of protection, were not chosen by mere whim. They were determined bearing in mind the economic and political requirements of the international economic order. Their objective was to keep surveillance on the actions of national governments so as to make possible the successful working of a competitive market economy. This meant that trade measures had to be stable over time and had to allow market forces to operate.[5] The above two norms follow naturally from these objectives.

There is a penchant to solve the sectoral problems by government intervention based on special arrangements with protectionist effects. Special treatment is no longer limited to textiles and agriculture. It has, of late, become institutionalised in steel, ship-building, synthetic fibres, automobiles, and to a lesser extent in consumer electronics, machine tools and a number of other more narrowly defined sectors. The voluntary export restrictions (VERs) and orderly marketing arrangements (OMAs) are the current modes of world trade in several of these sectors and product lines. Both of these NTBs are bilateral in nature and are in frequent use.

Who suffers most by the VERs and the OMAs? If the trading countries are arranged on a ladder according to their comparative advantage, it is easy to observe that the VERs and OMAs that are imposed by the industrialised countries are particularly biased against those countries which are just about to climb a rung of the ladder. Like the allocation of import quotas in LDCs, the export quotas are assigned to reflect 'historic and fair' shares. This mechanism favours the existing exporters at the expense of the more efficient newcomers. It is the newcomers who suffer most. With all these distorting practices in action, more international trade may be carried out today under the exceptions to the MFN principle than is carried out under the MFN principle itself. According to an UNCTAD estimate,[6] no more than 20 per cent of world trade is governed by the unconditional MFN principle. Another, more moderate estimate of free multilateral trade is 25 per cent of the total world trade.[7] There is no way of being precise on this count and these proportions may not be gospel truths, but are more or less correct. Few would argue that the GATT has been destroyed by bending to reality, yet it cannot be denied that the deviations have weakened the multilateral trading system.

Baneful as the erosive tendencies are, LDCs have been particularly penalised by them. The industrialised countries discriminated against the LDCs whenever they were disturbingly successful. The result was that their export volumes, terms of trade, and the purchasing power of their exports have been adversely affected. In sectors in which they had come to acquire international competitiveness, they found an array of NTBs – tariff rates are generally low – frustrating their exports. The discriminatory trade restrictions entangled their exports in managed trade mechanisms and reined them in. Furthermore, their exports are subjected to a variety of 'temporary' or 'emergency' protective devices, for dealing with market disruptions. If the new protectionism frustrates the converts among LDCs as they seek the benefits of their outward-oriented strategies, they might back track to their old policy regimes, thereby eroding the multilateral trading system further.

One of the many reasons for the erosion of the GATT framework is the emergence of new competitors. After 1970 the character of international trade changed; the trading world was no longer bi-polar (USA-EEC). Led by Japan and Korea (Republic of), there were several new entrants on the trade scene. The exports of the NICs have increased substantially in absolute terms, and their share in world exports also rose fast. Statistics in this regard have already been presented in Chapter 1. A second reason for the GATTs' weakening was, ironically, the enormous success of what it did best – multilateral tariff-cutting negotiations. The sharp postwar cuts in tariffs forced international trade relations onto the harder ground of the NTBs. These are inherently hard to measure and negotiate, and ill-defined by the GATT rules. When the Tokyo Round addressed some NTB-related issues, not all Contracting Parties accepted the obligations. Also, the enforcement procedures of the related codes proved to be slow, cumbersome and feeble.

The GATT also faced growing strains because the industrialised countries were beset with several economic difficulties. These economies were affected by slow-growth and high unemployment. They were emerging from two oil shocks and two bouts of recession. Decline in growth rates, and in the rate of investment in industrial economies, made structural adjustment a painful process and raised its short-term cost. This made adoption of sectoral measures sorely tempting. Compounding these problems in the early 1980s was the weakening of the American economy, due to, *inter alia*, an unanticipated rise in the value of the dollar. It went up 70 per cent during 1980-85, which was 40 per cent above the level where US firms were broadly competitive.[8] This made NTBs an attractive way out, in the process weakening the GATT discipline.

The authors of the GATT charter had assumed that the trade policies would be formulated and implemented against the background of stable currencies and co-ordinated international macroeconomic policies. However, the currencies have not been aligned and, as seen in the preceding paragraph, their values have shown large movements. Other macroeconomic variables have also not been synchronised. A salient example is the long enduring twin-deficits in the United States, which is a large trading partner of numerous LDCs. The erosion of the trading system is also the reflection of uncertainty and misalignment in the international economic system. The principal examples of the products that have been effectively removed from the application of the GATT principle and practices, and which in turn has eroded the multilateral trade discipline are agriculture, textiles and apparel and steel.

Agriculture

As economies grow, they tend to provide incentives for domestic agricultural production. The lower a country's comparative advantage in agriculture, the earlier it is forced to provide protection to its agriculture. A cross-country study reveals that the faster the growth rate of an economy, the faster is the decline in its agricultural comparative advantage.[9] Unlike the LDCs, which favour and protect their industrial sectors, agricultural protection has become a characteristic of most industrial market economies; the only exceptions are those economies that have managed to prevent a decline in their comparative advantage in agriculture. The degree of protection is linked to world market prices. Domestic food prices in Western Europe and Japan are often twice as high as the international prices. In most industrial countries agricultural trade policy has become an instrument to validate price support policies aimed at redistributing income to the agricultural sector.

Agricultural subsidies in the industrialised countries have reached monstrous proportions, and have made the trade in agricultural products increasingly restricted and distorted. The industrialised market economies also subside their agricultural exports and erect tariff barriers to protect their farm sector. The present costs of the support programmes are as follows: direct agricultural subsidies in the USA were $25 billion in 1986, $23 billion in the EEC, and $15 billion in Japan. The support programme costs include the cost of export subsidies.

The farmers in these countries have responded to these incentives by producing far more than the markets can absorb. Persistent overproduction has led to stockpiles of grain, beef and dairy products of record levels. Many of these products are sold in the international markets for less than their cost of production. Dumping of these surpluses on the world markets hurts the efficient non-subsidised farmers in countries like Argentina and Brazil. The US and EEC support for sugar producers has ruined many LDC farmers.

Although raw materials and many tropical agricultural products face relatively low levels of production in the industrialised countries, trade in agricultural products in general has caused a great number of problems since the birth of the GATT. Temperate and subtropical products face severe restrictions in the industrialised countries. This is partly because several products, like sugar, livestock and rice, are produced in both temperate and tropical regions. Also, tariffs escalate as the level of processing increases. Much of the trade in temperate and subtropical agricultural products is outside the GATT discipline, because the United States in the past and the EEC and Japan at present, have taken stands against it. They contended that domestic farm policy measures should not be subject to international limitations.[10] The United States agricultural trade was granted a waiver from the GATT discipline in 1954 and subsequently the Common Agricultural Policy (CAP) of the EEC was tacitly accepted.

During the last two decades agricultural trade has drifted towards bilateralism. The levels of protection of world trade in agriculture are presently higher than at the beginning of the Tokyo Round in 1973. The GATT appears willing to tolerate this. Recently 14 developed and developing countries have formed what is known as the Cairns Group[11] – named after the Australian town where they first met – to lobby for free trade in agriculture and for bringing it into the fold of the GATT. In 1987 the United States committed itself to eliminating all agricultural trade subsidies by the year 2000 – the so-called Zero-2000 proposal – but the EEC and Japan are still reluctant to take any steps beyond short-term measures. LDCs in the Cairns Group, for understandable reasons, consider that immediate steps have to be taken to reduce subsidies and that the date of Zero-2000 should be brought forward. The United States is willing to consider these proposals only if the EEC commits itself to a long-term reform.[12]

Textiles and Apparel

The trade in textiles and apparel is governed by an *ad hoc* arrangement called the multi-fibre arrangement (MFA). It is a sector-specific agreement made under the aegis of the GATT, and runs counter to its non-discriminatory principles. It sanctions bilaterally-negotiated quotas designed to slow down the growth of imports from the low-cost LDC producers to the industrialised country markets. The MFA is one of the most restrictive trade agreements. The first international cotton textiles agreement, namely, the Short-Term Cotton Textile Agreement, was set up in 1961. It was replaced by the Long-Term Agreement in 1962. Both were originally intended to be temporary measures. Their stated objective was to control disruption, and allow adjustment in industrial countries' markets stemming from imports from low-wage LDCs. At the same time they were supposed to provide LDCs with growing access to these markets. In due course, these agreements evolved into various MFAs, that is, MFA I (1974–77), MFA II (1978–81), MFA III (1982–86) and presently we are living in the reign of the MFA IV (1986–91). Thus, this temporary distraction is threatening to be permanent.[13]

Conceptually the MFAs are to strike a balance between the interests of the exporters and import-competing producers. But since the mid-1970s, this arrangement has become more restrictive. Annual growth rates of goods under quotas have generally been below the minimum specified 6 per cent. Successive MFAs have become less flexible, and more product categories have come under quantitative restrictions.[14]

The effect of such restrictions imposed by the industrial economies has been to create a marked break in the emerging pattern of trade with LDCs. In textiles, the share of the LDCs in the markets of the industrialised countries has not changed at all over the last two decades. This implies that considerable trade diversion has occurred. Since the restrictions under the MFAs are discriminatory, the purchases are diverted to producers who are as much likely to be located in another country as in the importing country itself. A result of the trade diversion was an increase in the market share of developed countries' (largely the EEC) exports to the United States after 1981. The trade diversion was substantial in the EEC as well; it was diverted to low-cost suppliers in southern Europe. Also, Italian exports to the rest of the EEC benefitted considerably from the EEC's protection against LDCs' exports.

Let the unwary be warned. A sectoral system of discriminatory protection tends to perpetuate itself and develop in the direction of greater restrictiveness. This follows from the political process that motivates its design. The MFAs are no exception to this.

Steel

Due to the adoption of new technology, a major shift occurred in the international competitiveness of steel production in the 1970's, which led to a shift in the comparative advantage. This was a period of sharp fall in demand. Since steel is a highly capital-intensive industry, some developed countries were faced with choosing between introducing massive structural adjustment programmes and introducing protective measures like heavy subsidisation to maintain grossly inefficient production. The major steel producing countries chose the latter approach. To avoid recourse to safeguards or renegotiation procedures – both of which require compensation or permit retaliation under Articles XIX and XXIII – they resorted to a variety of other mechanism outside the GATT framework, which include the use of NTBs like the VERs and the OMAs. The result is the birth of a system of managed trade in steel, in which the most competitive new entrants to the world steel market – which are generally LDCs – have no say whatsoever.

Economic Integration

At present there are several customs unions and free trade areas in the world. The largest and the most important, the EEC, has been enlarged to 12 countries. The newly formed free-trade arrangement between the United States and Canada is the latest (January 1988) in a series of about 40 such arrangements notified to the GATT. The customs unions and free-trade areas undermine the multilateral approach to world trade. Taken to extreme, this tendency would lead to pairs or small groups of countries seeking narrow advantages for themselves in restructuring their trade with third parties. Such formations have an ambiguous effect on world trade and welfare. The formation of unions abolishes trade barriers among the members, which creates new trade flows between them. But the union erects a common tariff wall which discriminates against the rest of the

world. Goods which were formerly bought from non-members
would be replaced by those which are perhaps more expensively
produced substitutes from other members of the union. Thus,
trade diversion is a strong possibility.

Article XXIV of the GATT does allow customs unions and
free-trade agreements, but only as long as they do not raise
trade barriers to third parties. None of the existing agreements – least of all the EEC – has emerged from GATT's
scrutiny with a clean bill of health. Typically, considerable
amounts of trade diversion take place and outsiders are
penalised.

4   RECIPROCITY AND GRADUATION

Reciprocity implies that a country receiving trade concessions is
obliged to provide equivalent benefit to the providing country.
In practice, it has not been possible to have an equal degree of
reciprocity between trading partners. Yet, an imprecise application of this principle has worked as a potent force for the
progressive liberalisation of the trading system of the industrialised countries in the successive rounds of the MTNs. The
negotiations are based on first-difference reciprocity, which
means reciprocity or balancing of tariff concessions at the
margin.

I have mentioned how the LDCs have made use of the
provisions of Article XVIII and other exceptions allowed under
Part IV of the GATT charter. The benefits they derived were
only from the negotiations of reciprocal concessions among the
industrialised countries, and the generalisation of these concessions to apply to the Contracting Parties under the MFN
umbrella. In Chapter 3 we have seen how the LDCs benefitted
far less than the major industrial market economies from the
various rounds of MTNs. They have continued to face relatively
higher tariffs on products of particular interest to them in
international trade. Certain persisting adverse features of the
structure of protectionism in industrial countries, like escalation
of tariffs with the stages of processing, could have been
modified if the LDCs had participated more fully in the
negotiations on the basis of some qualified principle of reciprocity. According to the GATT data, the trade of the LDCs affected

by Kennedy and Tokyo Rounds added up to about $3 billion and $40 billion, respectively. In contrast, the total international trade affected by these rounds was $40 billion and $155 billion, respectively. Another proof of the disproportionate benefits is that the present US tariffs on textile mill products, apparel and leather products are 12.4 per cent, 20.0 per cent and 9.3 per cent, respectively. Compared to this, the average tariffs on manufactured products are 4.9 per cent.

The economic rationale of the principle of reciprocity is simple. The first gain that reciprocity brings to an LDC is the liberalisation of its domestic economy, which in turn improves its resource allocation. By adhering to strict non-reciprocity, the LDCs have relinquished an important instrument for fighting down their domestic protectionist forces and in that missed an opportunity to rationalise their own economic structures. The second, and greater, gain occurs when LDCs' own trade barriers are brought down within the context of a worldwide move toward open markets. Thus, the negative consequences of not participating in the reciprocity concept are more than mere limitations on improvement in access to markets in the industrial countries.

During the decade of the 1970s the importance of LDCs as world markets soared. The nominal value of their imports from the rest of the world increased; the average annual growth rate for the decade was 23.7 per cent. By 1985 the exports of manufactures from the industrialised to the developing countries had reached 28.1 per cent of their manufactured exports to the developed countries. In case of the United States, exports to LDCs constituted 25.8 per cent of total exports. In volume terms it was almost equal to US exports to the EEC and Japan combined. For the EEC, exports to LDCs represent 31.3 per cent of total extra-EEC exports, and greatly exceed exports to the United States and Japan.[15] This steady growth of LDC markets has occurred despite significant protection in the markets of LDCs. Since the importance of LDCs in world trade has increased, they should *a fortiori* participate in a symmetrical manner in the trade negotiations. This has been expounded in more detail in Chapter 6.

Of late, the theme of graduation has tended to dominate discussions in international trade fora. This concept was spelled out clearly in the Tokyo Round decisions. It maintains that as

with economic growth the capacity of LDCs to make contributions and negotiate settlements improves, so would their ability
'to participate more fully in the framework of rights and
obligations under the General Agreement'.[16] It is reasonable to
expect the more economically advanced LDCs, like the NICs, to
open up their markets over time and to begin the process of
fuller integration into the international trading community. The
initiatives to be taken by the NICs in this regard are dealt with
in Chapter 6. One aspect of such integration is the gradual
phasing down of the 'special and differential treatment' that the
more advanced LDCs now receive, and the progressive alignment of their own trade policies with the GATT provisions
generally applicable to the industrialised countries. Ironically,
at present several LDCs which are the prime candidates for
being graduated are either (1) under dire financial pressures, or
(2) facing increased discrimination in the industrialised countries on the grounds of being low-cost suppliers. In turn, they
feel that they are being prematurely graduated and resent it
vocally.

5 DEFENSIVE ADJUSTMENTS UNDER THE SAFEGUARD CLAUSE

During the conduct of international trade unforeseen emergen-
cies may arise, which may call for provision for release of a
country from its multilateral obligations for a limited period.
Article XIX is such an emergency safeguard clause of the GATT
charter. It allows a country to impose defensive emergency
measures if a sudden surge of imports threatens its domestic
industry. It is an 'escape clause' and has been fashioned for
adjustment to import competition. The safeguard clause is
intended to allow the importing country time for reallocation of
resources. To this end, the importing Contracting Party shall be
free 'to suspend the relevant obligation, in whole or in part, or
to withdraw or modify the concessions in respect of the
product, to the extent, and for such time as may be necessary to
prevent or remedy such injury'.[17] This action could only be
taken after consultation with the exporting country and inform-
ing the GATT. In the absence of consultation, the exporting
country can take retaliatory measures after 90 days.[18] The

nature and extent of the retaliatory action is to be determined by the extent to which the exporting country loses by the use of safeguard controls by the importing country. Further, any action taken under the safeguard clause has to conform to the most-favoured-nation principle. In sum, the safeguard action can only be temporarily resorted to in an emergency, and in a non-discriminatory manner.

With the emergence of the NICs as successful exporters in several lines of manufactures, structural changes occurred in international trade. The exports of the NICs were not large in relative terms, but they were concentrated in specific product lines and markets. The NICs had comparative advantage in them, which they sagaciously exploited by producing at low cost and exporting. This resulted in a rapid rate of increase in import penetration in many industrial country markets, which generated pressure on the industrial economies to adjust structurally and keep their economies aligned with their own shifting comparative advantage.

Article XIX permits the use of either a tariff or a quota. As seen below, quotas, which are more restrictive, have been far more popular than tariff measures:

Table 4.1   TARIFFS AND QUOTA MEASURES USED UNDER ARTICLE XIX

	Tariff measures	Quantitative restrictions	Total	Ratio of quantitative restrictions to total
1949–58	13	3	16	19
1959–68	20	16	36	44
1969–86	15	28	43	65
1979–86	17	25	42	60

SOURCE   World Bank, *World Development Report, 1987* (New York: Oxford University Press, 1987) p. 161.

The most recent trend in this regard is that when efficient imports exerted pressure on their domestic industries, instead of petitioning for protection under Article XIX, the industrialised countries preferred to ignore the provisions of Article XIX and take illegal action outside the GATT discipline. The LDCs, particularly the NICs, found themselves highly vulnerable to this action. It was generally taken outside the GATT. LDCs did not pose a realistic retaliatory threat because of (1) the small size of their markets, and (2) the low elasticity of their imports. Only a few of the large LDCs – Argentina, Brazil, China, India, Indonesia, Malaysia, Mexico, South Korea and Taiwan – could threaten to cut imports and thereby inflict some damage on an offending industrial nation.

Having shelved the use of Article XIX, the industrial countries created an alternative set of rules (for example, the MFA), or they used illegal discriminatory import controls (for example, QRs) or extra-legal ones (for example, VERs). The principal reason for shying away from using Article XIX was not economic but political. The importing countries chose to offend because of the non-discriminatory requirement of the safeguard clause. It implied taking action against established trading partners, whose rates of growth of exports may have been rather stable, and where a realistic possibility of retaliation was high. They saw no reason to injure exporters who were causing no problems when there was a need to deal with one exporting country, whose exports were disrupting their domestic industry.[19] As the argument goes, the MFN requirement is the main reason behind the recent drift of the industrial countries towards the VERs and the OMAs. If it is waived, the VERs would disappear by themselves. The argument is fallacious. Translated, it implies that if abrogating the GATT code is made acceptable, no one would contravene it.

The offending countries pay a high cost of drifting into the VERs, because their economic cost is more than that of an import quota. Primarily, they raise consumer prices and distort resource allocation. In addition, they transfer rents to foreigners by allowing them to hike their export prices. For the exporter, the profits per unit of exports rise in the restricted market. The country using VERs suffers in terms of trade decline. In spite of this, ostensibly, governments prefer VERs to the legitimate use of Article XIX. The GATT statistics show that since 1978 VERs have outnumbered safeguard actions by more than 8 to 1.

5 The Policy Blueprint

INTRODUCTION

This chapter sets forth not an 'ideal', but *à la* William Cline a 'constrained ideal', of a trading regime for the LDCs. The ideal regime, like perfect competition, may only be notional. It may, indeed, result in optimal resource allocation, but be difficult to put in place. In what follows, we shall try to look at the domestic and international aspects of the international trade strategy for LDCs as well as at the role of the international institutions.

1. THE DOMESTIC DIMENSIONS

From an Illiberal to a Liberal Strategy

It has been set out that LDCs have followed highly protective policies and that high tariff barriers are ubiquitous. The web of NTBs like foreign exchange licensing, import licensing in different products, canalisation and special taxes on imports, work as effective barriers to trade. All these add up to create distortions in the domestic policy regime – sometimes even without being detected – and take it away from liberal, market-oriented efficient policies. The role of the price-mechanism is diluted and incentives no longer remain neutral, leading to sub-optimal resource allocation. The costs of a distorted economic regime to the national welfare are diffused but high.

In most LDCs government intervention in economic affairs is extensive; it affects the capital market, the trade regime and indeed almost every aspect of the economy. Government policies, when found deficient, are not altered readily. They change slowly, if at all. In fact, when regulations and controls do not yield the desired results, they are not abolished but tightened. When the subsidies do not produce the intended outcome, they are raised and the policy continues.[1] A classic illustration of this falacy is the Indian economy in its bureaucratic clutches. Deepak Lal has sagaciously observed, between a necessarily imperfect planning mechanism and a necessarily imperfect market mechanism, the latter is likely to perform better in practice.[2]

The LDCs with high incidence of protection, and therefore high domestic distortion, are particularly concentrated in South Asia and East Africa. Salient among these are Ethiopia, Kenya, Bangladesh, India and Pakistan. Effective protection rates of 100+ per cent are easily found in these LDCs. Several Latin American LDCs had high rates of protection in the 1950s, examples being Argentina, Brazil, Chile and Uruguay. Interestingly, they had scaled them down by the early 1970s. LDCs with a tradition of low incidence of protection are Chile, Korea (Republic of), Malawi, Malaysia, Mexico, Taiwan and Yugoslavia. The range of protection rates indicates the scale of discrimination between different industries. As noted earlier, the countries with the lowest incidence of protection are Hong Kong, Kuwait and Singapore.

In the recent past several LDCs have endeavoured to move towards a liberal policy regime and bring down the level of distortion. Mexico and Brazil have done so by correcting their severe currency overvaluation. In accordance with their adjustment programmes, they are moving towards reducing reliance on NTBs and rationalising their tariff structures. The QRs have also been brought down in India and Pakistan. In Thailand and Turkey trade liberalisation included reduction in both tariff and non-tariff barriers, and in Malaysia tariffs were curbed. Korea (Republic of) is proceeding with its phased liberalisation programme, and the height of its tariff was to be approximately the same as that in the OECD countries by the end of 1988.[3] In addition several LDCs have undertaken to reduce or freeze their export subsidies under the GATT code on subsidies.

There is a significant association between distortion and growth performance. Statistical analysis of a sample of 34 LDCs confirms this hypothesis. The distortions in the domestic trade regime explain 11.0 per cent of the variation in growth performance. The time horizon of this study was 1971–81. The group averages of countries with high, medium and low distortions for GDP growth, domestic savings rate, return on investment, growth rate of agriculture, manufacturing and export volume are presented in the table below:

Table 5.1 DOMESTIC DISTORTIONS AND GROWTH
PERFORMANCE (in per cent)

	High	Medium	Low	Average
1. GDP growth rate	3.9	5.3	6.1	5.0
2. Domestic Savings ratio	12.4	19.9	19.6	17.4
3. Return on Investment	22.0	23.4	24.6	23.2
4. Growth rate of Industry	4.7	6.3	7.8	6.1
5. Growth rate of agriculture	1.9	3.5	3.4	3.0
6. Growth rate of Export volume	0.7	3.6	9.5	3.6

SOURCE Agarwala (1983). Table – 2.

The table above clearly demonstrates the effect of high protection on the growth of the industrial sector and exports. For the overall growth rate and the efficiency of investment, protectionist policy seems to make a difference. For savings, however, the negative association between the degree of protection and performance is there, but the signals are not clear.

The infant-industry argument for protection in the LDCs is justified on the grounds of 'learning by doing', that is, productivity improves as a function of the cumulative volume of output. This argument is also accepted as a rationale for intervention on the grounds of creation of externalities and the 'dynamic effects'. But as seen in Chapter 3, this argument is based on two weak premises. Besides, if an infant industry is to be protected it should be protected not just for sales in the domestic market but also for exporting. So if the industry has to be promoted it should be provided with, say, infrastructural support or subsidised factors of production. Unlike tariffs and QRs such assistance does not discriminate between the home market and export markets.

The period of infant-industry protection should be decided and publicised for every industry in advance. After the stipulated period is over, the tariff wall should be gradually scaled down, brick by brick. LDCs must discourage those infant industries which prefer not to grow up to be internationally competitive. Also, it is taken for granted that the process of bringing down the tariff wall would spawn some industrial morality; the LDCs should stoically accept this because it may be the manifestation of the fact that the comparative advantage of the economy does not lie in the dying sectors but somewhere else. A liberal or free trade regime would *inter alia* bring the domestic price structure of LDCs close to that in the international market. It would also help in identifying the leading sectors and sub-sectors of the economy and enhance its ability and keenness to compete.

As noted in Chapter 3, one of the main reasons for applying protectionist measures is the current account deficit. It was also emphasised that since we are now in a flexible exchange rate regime, this argument is not wholly valid. The exchange rate should be used as a device for switching demand away from imported goods to home produced goods. Trade restrictions should be eschewed like evil for current account balancing purposes. The Cambridge Economic Policy group[5] did not agree, nor did most of the Latin American economists, who argued that the effects of devaluation work with a lag and therefore import restrictions should be preferred at a time of a balance of payments crisis. It should be noted that quantitative restrictions also take time to implement, because usually an elaborate administrative structure is needed for them. Besides, if there is no price control over the restricted items, the restrictions would yield a quota-rent to import-licence holders. Such cases would promote vigorous rent seeking. Once the import restrictions are in place, they are slow to go – if they go at all. This would imply a medium- and long-term adverse effect through failure to stimulate exports. The import pattern would also be distorted as a non-market method is used to determine what to import, when and how much.[6]

The success potential of a liberal policy regime is fully explained by the neo-classical paradigm. The logic of trade liberalisation is that tariffs should be as low as possible. As long as the average tariff is not zero, an element of discrimination against exports remains – unless they are equivalently subsidised. However, in a real life situation, beyond the infant-industry stage, protection and, therefore, distortions in the domestic policy regime must be kept at a low ebb. The question, then, arises: how low is low? Once the infant-industry phase is over, the upper limit for effective protection should be

40 per cent.[7] This is because high protection limits competition in sheltered domestic markets; it inhibits specialisation and promotes risk aversion among managers and entrepreneurs. Although an upper limit of effective protection has been suggested, some LDCs with a tradition of low incidence of protection have done better and have brought the limit down to 30 per cent. Recently, Chile achieved a tariff level of 10 per cent. Subsequently, it was revised to a uniform tariff of 20 per cent.

In order to minimise the efficiency losses and economic distortions, the trade policy instruments have to be reformed. The first step of a liberalisation strategy is replacing NTBs by tariffs. Quantitative restrictions (QRs) are frequently used in LDCs for restricting trade, largely because they do so severely. The move from QRs to tariffs is a healthy one because the latter are relatively less protective than the former. More importantly, a tariff is a price instrument, a QR is not; therefore, the former is more transparent and the changes in international prices feed through more readily into the domestic economy. The knowledge of and link with international prices is essential for domestic producers. Not knowing the relative costs of imports, domestic producers cannot commit themselves to production for exports. The conditions under which they have to compete in the international markets become a matter of conjecture for them. Furthermore, quotas confer a degree of monopoly power over domestic producers, who may then lower output, whereas tariffs encourage production. Also, quotas are allocated inefficiently by the bureaucracy, which creates deadweight losses that could be avoided by using tariffs. The costs of implementing quotas and tariffs differ, with the former being more costly to administer than the latter.

Replacing the QRs with tariffs has been the key element in the early stages of trade policy reform. In some cases this has been the only element. For instance, recently Greece and Israel removed almost all quotas and replaced them with tariffs. Sri Lanka went through this exercise in the late 1970s. For the most part the tariffs were lower than the tariff equivalent of the QRs. The results were highly beneficial. Production increased in the formerly protected sectors, as firms began to operate in a less restrictive and more transparent regime. The economic growth rate speeded up.

The second relevant step towards openness and greater neutrality of the trade regime entails (1) lowering the average level of protection and (2) reducing the average dispersion, or variance, of protection. If the dispersion is not reduced, as the average tariff declines, the tariff structure may become less neutral and more discriminatory, and therefore, highly distorting. A trade policy reform that reduces tariffs on intermediate capital goods but leaves those on finished products intact – a common phenomenon in LDCs – ends up increasing effective protection, even though it reduces the average level of tariffs. To diminish the average tariff levels as well as their dispersion, LDCs can apply the following measures:

(1)   an equi-proportional cut in all tariffs;
(2)   an equi-proportional reduction of the excess of each tariff over some target level;
(3)   higher proportional reductions of higher tariffs.

An appropriate combination of the above three measures can also be profitably utilised.[8]

Every LDC has a few shibboleths which are impossible to overcome in the short term. The policy-makers should work around them and try to ease the burden of adjustment. An obvious step is to phase the liberalisation measures over several years. The Tokyo Round allowed a transitional phase of eight years. The next step is to provide adjustment assistance direct to the injured parties, that is, the firm and the workforce. The injured firms can be provided with subsidised capital or some of their outstanding debt can be absorbed by the government. Paying some kind of insurance premium for the trade-related plant closures could also be considered. The workers can be given retraining and relocation allowances. In the NBER studies,[9] there is evidence that after a successful liberalisation, which accompanies devaluation, exports first decline and then start climbing. They follow the J-curve pattern. This phenomenon was documented for liberalisation episodes in several LDCs. For example, the June 1966 Indian devaluation and liberalisation policy package showed this type of export pattern.

Experience suggests that simply drawn schemes are more functional than the fine-tuning kind, which deal with tariffs on a sector-by-sector basis. Some trade economists prefer the concertina approach to tariff cutting. This entails cutting all tariffs above a certain ceiling, then all tariffs above the new, lower ceiling are lowered to that ceiling, and so on.[10] The advantage of the concertina method is that it yields the lowest adjustment costs without leading to inadvertent increases in effective protection. During the 1970s Chile by and large followed this line of tariff reductions.

As regards the question of ideal time span in which to complete the reforms, there is no unanimity among trade economists. Some of the better publicised trade policy reforms – in South Korea and the countries of Southern Europe – took as long as two decades. A few have been completed in the medium term, for instance, in Chile the process lasted for five years. Completing this work in the short term has been found to be implausible. If the reforms are carried out briskly, say, in the medium-term, they would be more credible and entail less adjustment costs.

Import Substitution Versus Export Promotion

The age-old war between the import-substitutionists and the export-promotionists is still raging, with the proponents of the latter appearing to be the victors. The exposition in Chapter 2 strongly suggests that of the two trade regimes export promotion would have significant implications for long-term economic growth; it has now come to be the new orthodoxy in trade economies.

The two regimes confront the entrepreneur with radically different signals and incentives. There is convincing evidence that the high effective protection rates that go with import-substitution regimes impose high economic costs. These costs affect the structure of incentives, and industries are discriminated against, which has a distorting influence on the efficiency of resource allocation. The *World Development Report 1987* studied the macroeconomic performance of four groups of developing countries for two periods ranging between 1963-73 and 1973-85. It took a large sample of 41 LDCs. When the following macroeconomic indicators were monitored: real GDP growth rate, gross domestic savings, real GDP per capita, the ICOR, rate of inflation and the rate of growth of manufactured

Table 5.2   GROWTH OF GDP, INPUTS AND TOTAL FACTOR PRODUCTIVITY

Trade strategy and period		Average growth of GDP	Total factor productivity		Factor inputs		
			Growth rate	Share in GDP growth	Growth of capital	Growth of labor	Share of total inputs in GDP growth
Strongly outward oriented							
Hong Kong	1960–70	9.10	4.28	47.0	7.60	2.97	53.0
Korea, Republic of	1960–73	9.70	4.10	42.3	6.60	5.00	57.7
Singapore	1972–80	8.00	−0.01	−0.1	9.48	5.52	100.1
Moderately outward oriented							
Brazil	1960–74	7.30	1.60	21.9	7.50	3.30	78.1
Colombia	1960–74	5.60	2.10	37.5	3.90	2.80	62.5
Israel	1960–65	11.00	3.40	30.9	13.10	5.00	69.1
Moderately inward oriented							
Mexico	1960–74	5.60	2.10	37.5	3.90	2.80	62.5
Strongly inward oriented							
Argentina	1960–74	4.10	0.70	17.1	3.80	2.20	82.9
Chile	1960–74	4.40	1.20	27.3	4.20	1.90	72.7
India	1959/60–1978/79	6.24	−0.18	−2.9	4.77	1.65	102.9
Peru	1960–70	5.30	1.50	28.3	4.40	2.70	71.7
Turkey	1963–75	6.40	2.23	34.8	6.82	1.02	65.2

NB   Total factor productivity is defined as the growth of GDP above and beyond the growth in the use of both labour and capital inputs

SOURCE   Chenery, Hollis, Sherman Robinson and Moshe Syrquim. *Industrialization and Growth: A Comparative Study* (New York: Oxford University Press, 1986) pp. 20–1

exports, the first group of LDCs displayed a spectacular performance, way ahead of the other three.[11] The postwar experience
of productivity growth in LDCs underlines the relevance of
trade policy. Table 5.2 presents statistics regarding factor
productivity and factor growth in selected LDCs. It shows that
the total factor productivity increased much faster in the
strongly outward-oriented economies than in the strongly
inward-oriented ones.

A policy shift from import-substitution to export-promotion
should generate additional real income by raising income
through the multiplier effect, as rising exports bring spare
capacity into use. Since in LDCs the marginal propensity to save
is higher than the average propensity to save, additional real
income would increase the average propensity to save. Another
link between trade policy and savings is that, since a higher-
than-average part of the income generated by exports is saved,
domestic savings rise further.

Prerequisites for an Outward-Oriented Strategy

Generalisations on this count are slow to emerge, yet Anne
Krueger's researches into the behaviour of the four East Asian
NICs have led her to some clear-cut policy conclusions. She has
identified several prerequisites that must be present if an
export-promotion trade policy is to succeed. Admittedly, not all
the prerequisites need to be in place for the adoption of the
strategy. Besides, there are always shortcomings in the implementation of the optimal policies because markets are never
perfect. Nevertheless, some policy measures have been enume-
rated as prerequisites. This is not to conclude that no other
factors than the prerequisites set forth in the following paragraph would assist in policy implementation. There would
always be relevant country-specific and period-specific
measures that would come in handy.

The salient prerequisites are as follows: first, in trade policy
governments cannot build a half-way house. They cannot be
half-oriented towards import substitution and half-oriented
toward export promotion. The government has consciously to
choose between outward-orientation and rewards and incentives for firms' performance in the international market, or

inward-orientation and the rewards that firms get by operating in sheltered domestic markets. Second, the commitment to export-oriented policies should be clear and well-publicised, that is, the economic agents have to understand that the government would continue to make exporting profitable. Third, the financial markets should guarantee that export-oriented sectors will receive timely finance at domestically competitive interest rates. Fourth, a realistic exchange rate is indispensable for an export-oriented policy to succeed. The real exchange rate should be stable over time. Fifth, quantitative restrictions and the export-promotion strategy do not go together. There should not be any quantitative intervention in any aspect of international trade. Sixth, exporting industries should have ready access to international markets for the importables needed in their manufacturing process.[12] Exporters should operate under a regime close to free trade.

Piecing the evidence together, one can conclude that rapid economic growth is associated with an outward-oriented trade regime. The evidence from the four Asian super-exporters suggests that economies can attain a high level of performance efficiency and rapid economic growth under this regime in a relatively short span of time. LDCs that have followed an import-substitution regime have performed poorly. A policy shift from import substitution to export promotion is a politically difficult process. The shift, however, could be best begun with (1) devaluing the exchange rate to an appropriate level, (2) swapping tariffs for the QRs, and (3) lowering the average effective protection in the economy. Once the transition period is over, the outward-oriented policy regime creates a momentum of its own and is relatively easier to sustain. As opposed to this, the rival regime needs constant attention to keep it from collapse.

Exchange Rates

High inflation rates are endemic in LDCs, which implies that the real values of their currencies decline and they become overvalued. This, in turn, leads to a loss of general competitiveness in the international markets. To offset this loss, the LDCs are forced to devalue – or depreciate, if the currency is on a floating exchange rate. This keeps the real exchange rate constant. The real exchange rate here is taken to be an index of relative domestic and world prices expressed in terms of a common currency.

The effective exchange rate or the nominal effective exchange rate is a trade-weighted index of the bilateral exchange rates between the domestic currency and the currencies of the trading partners. Only a certain number of principal or large trading partners are taken into account. Somewhat less narrow and more relevant is the concept of real effective exchange rate (REER), which is the nominal effective exchange rate, adjusted for the differences in the inflation rates between the domestic economy and those of the trading partners, or it is the purchasing-power-adjusted effective exchange rate. The REER is the most accurate measure of changes in an LDC's price competitiveness against its trading partners. If the rate of inflation of the principal trading partners is relatively low, the LDC soon finds its REER misaligned with those of its trading partners. The trading partners gain at the expense of the LDC. The alternative is to let its currency float to minimise the adverse effects of inflation. However, what most LDCs do is use controls to prop up their overvalued exchange rates. They should avoid exchange controls like the plague. In order to achieve neutral status and compensate for the currency over-valuation, some LDCs provide compensatory export incentives. The Korean government has consciously maintained stability in REER by means of periodic devaluations and compensating for currency overvaluation through tax and financial export incent-ives. Therefore, the compensated exchange rate for exports becomes the nominal exchange rate, minus the compensation for currency overvaluation per dollar of exports.

In international trade, most LDCs are what is called 'small countries' because they cannot affect the world prices of traded goods. A depreciating REER raises the relative prices of trad-ables which encourages their production and discourages ex-ports. This provides a measure of incentive to move into the production of non-tradables and out of tradables. This interpre-tation is relevant and useful to bear in mind when looking at the effect of changing trade and macroeconomic policies on the structure of incentives and production.

Excessive variability in the REER creates an uncertain climate for investment and skews the structure of incentives. If the nominal exchange rate is adjusted as frequently as the need arises and stable macroeconomic policies are followed, the REER would remain constant and stable. Exchange rate policy is crucial, and is a powerful and simple instrument for promoting exports. In addition, it would be wholesome for an LDC to curb its domestic inflation sufficiently to make it possible to peg the currency to a suitable foreign currency, to SDRs, or some other pragmatic basket of currencies.

2. THE INTERNATIONAL DIMENSIONS

Progressing towards Freer Trade

For its welfare implications to the international economy, it is imperative to progress towards an open, liberal trading order. This has far reaching implications both for the industrialised and the developing economies. The responsibility for devising and maintaining such a trading order, and resisting the surge in protectionism, rests somewhat unevenly on the two country groups, with the former sharing more of it than the latter. The next related policy target should be the 'rolling back' of protection, in particular that which is in the form of NTBs. Opportunities exist for both the country groups to cut down on existing trade barriers and to adjust domestic policies that inhibit trade on a multilateral basis. Growth-oriented adjustment in the industrial economies and growth-oriented adjustment in the developing economies reinforce each other, and continually benefit both the country groups. Both country groups should accept this course of action because it is a non-zero-sum game, one which would eventually benefit all the players in the international trade arena. In addition, liberalised trade is the most politically viable alternative to 'aid'. However, past experience suggests that good economics is politically unsellable.

Expressions like 'roll-back' and 'standstill' have become part of GATT parlance, and refer to measures inconsistent with the provisions of the GATT charter. At the time of UNCTAD VI,[13] the industrialised economies agreed to work systematically towards reducing or eliminating quantitative restrictions and measures having similar effects. There were other occasions when industrial economies committed themselves to rolling back trade-restrictive measures. In Punta del Este,[14] similar holy intentions were repeated. Some relaxation of non-tariff measures has taken place in some industrial economies, yet protectionism has not shown any signs of abating. The relaxations were too modest and were outweighed by new measures.

That there are benefits to be had from multilateral trade liberalisation can be seen from the use of a trade model simulating such liberalisation. With the help of one such model, the UNCTAD secretariat has estimated the effects of full MNF liberalisation of both tariffs and NTBs in the EEC, Japan and the United States, for non-fuel trade. This simulation exercise estimated that EEC imports (excluding the intra-trade) would expand by $32.2 billion from a base of $171.2 billion, while Japanese imports would grow by $9.4 billion from a base of $65.1 billion and US imports by $33.7 billion from a base of $184.2 billion. The exercise was based on 1983 statistics and the reported results are in 1983 dollars. The welfare costs of protection were of the order of $1.9 billion in the EEC, $1.0 billion in Japan and $1.5 billion in the USA. As expected, the major costs are associated with the highly protected clothing and agriculture sectors, which are of particular export interest to LDCs.[15]

Empirical attempts have also been made to reckon the cost of these programmes for consumers and producers. For instance, the values of direct subsidies for the agricultural support programmes in the EEC, Japan and the USA have already been reported. However, much larger are the costs borne by consumers and tax payers. A World Bank study estimated the annual domestic costs and benefits of agricultural protection to consumers, tax payers and producers.[16] The estimates given in Table 5.3 below are not precise, but they do give an indication of the massive volume of transfers involved. The transfer, in this case, is defined as the average loss to consumers and tax payers per dollar transferred to producers.

The table shows that in every case, producers gain less than consumers and that tax payers lose. The higher transfer ratio for Japan reflects higher levels of protection. The tax payer costs, however, are lower for Japan. To be sure, Japan spends a substantial sum on subsidies but its import restraints on balance provide revenue through tariff collections. From the table one

Table 5.3 ANNUAL DOMESTIC COSTS AND BENEFITS
OF AGRICULTURAL PROTECTION
(In billions of $)

	Consumer costs	+ Taxpayer costs	− Producer benefits	= Total domestic costs	Transfer Ratio
1. EEC	34.6	11.5	30.7	15.4	1.50
2. Japan	7.1	−0.4	2.6	4.1	2.58
3. USA	5.7	10.3	11.6	4.4	1.38

SOURCE The World Bank, *World Development Report, 1986*
(Washington, DC: 1986). Table 6.5.

can infer that agricultural protection is an expensive way to
transfer income between various sections of society. In Japan
consumers and tax payers lost $2.58 for every $1.00 transferred
to producers. If the trade were liberalised, this resource waste
could be avoided.

The protectionist drift should, therefore, be stalled. The
sectors which are in the clutches of protectionism should be
liberalised in a phased manner. For the negotiations to be
meaningful to LDCs, inclusion of (1) the MFA, (2) the VERs in
steel and (3) protection in agricultural trade are of great
importance. The ultimate objective of the negotiations in these
issues should be to bring them under the umbrella of the
General Agreement.

The next tangle relates to the NTBs. Little negotiating
experience exists within the GATT system to deal with this
issue. But there are some precedents which portend a plausible
answer. In the late 1940s and 1950s some European countries
undertook simultaneous reductions in quantitative restrictions,
according to mutually agreed formulae. Also, Japan liberalised
its NTB regime under a negotiated formula. Furthermore, the
IMF and the World Bank have argued LDCs into systematically
eliminating quantitative restrictions.

Developing Countries in the Trade Negotiations:
an Asymmetry

An imbalance exists in the process of lowering tariff and
non-tariff barriers by LDCs and the industrial market econo-

mies. The industrial economies mutually bargain for reciprocal trade concessions. LDCs, however, do not trade concessions with the industrial economies, or with each other, during the various MTNs, but frequently undertake reductions in trade barriers unilaterally, under the direction of the World Bank, or while following a 'conditionality' package prescribed by the IMF. Sometimes good economic sense dawns on them and they liberalise their trade regimes of their own accord. Several NICs, middle-income LDCs and some large LDCs, like India, have taken decisive trade liberalisation measures during the 1970s and 1980s.

Despite undertaking unilateral reductions, LDCs manage to appear as non-participants in the multilateral exchange of trade concessions.[17] Ways must be found to systematically recognise the liberalisation measures already undertaken by LDCs, and equate them with the concessions given by the industrial economies at the time of the negotiations under the auspices of the GATT. LDCs could be provided with 'credit' for liberalisation measures adopted unilaterally, or under the Bank or Fund programmes. However, it needs to be conceded that the evaluation of past unilateral liberalisations may seem inadequate to induce the industrialised countries to reduce their NTBs in areas of interest to LDCs. In the event that the industrial countries are willing to undertake such concessions, LDCs – in particular the NICs and the middle-income LDCs – should be willing to offer some reciprocal reductions in their own tariff and non-tariff barriers. This reduction would, eventually, stimulate balanced long-term growth in LDCs.[18]

In effect, this implies gradually shedding the special and discriminatory status enjoyed currently by the LDCs, and participating in international trade as equal partners on equal terms. To be sure, not all LDCs can be expected to do this. The NICs, however, can make a good beginning in this regard, and can be drawn more fully into the GATT system.

Intra-trade among Developing Countries

Intra-developing country trade is another possible direction for trade expansion, though a decline has been observed in it during the 1980s. This trend needs to be arrested and reversed. To this end, LDCs should negotiate some functional scheme of preferences with each other based on the principle of mutuality of advantages, to benefit all the participants equitably. In this context one can ill afford to forget that the experience of LDCs with regional and sub-regional preferential trading arrangements has been disappointing. While negotiating they should take into account their respective levels of economic and industrial development, the pattern of their comparative advantage and trade policies. The negotiating LDCs should also focus on each other's tariffs, para-tariffs and non-tariff measures.[19] It has been noted in Chapter 1 that there is no conflict in exporting to both the developing and industrialised economies. Such a strategy is preferable because it would enable LDCs to find markets for both high- and low-skill exportables. Negotiating a scheme would not be an easy task, because a good deal of empirical information needed for this purpose is not available. For instance, credible data on the levels of protection, the pervasiveness of NTBs, information on the volume and composition of intra-developing country trade, and the estimates of LDCs' supply and demand elasticities, are not easily available. Recent data collection efforts, however, have filled some gaps. A simulation exercise was attempted to see whether a kind of GSP among LDCs could be of benefit. It simulates the likely increases in intra-trade that would occur under different margins of tariff preferences. The results show that, with an infinitely elastic supply, a full tariff preference, that is, a 100 per cent tariff cut, could hike intra-trade by as much as $14 billion per year.[20] This represents a 17 per cent increase over the present level. The exercise also demonstrated the importance of negotiating a meaningful tariff margin; a 10 per cent reduction in tariff would only produce a trade expansion of between $800 million and $1.4 billion, depending on the supply conditions.[21] Trade gains of this magnitude are indeed meagre. The LDCs should bring down their tariff barriers unilaterally or according to a predetermined medium-term plan. An identical approach for dismantling the NTBs would go a long way.

The projections show that some LDCs, in particular those in Africa, would be able to increase their exports only marginally. This would occur simultaneously with a sizeable growth in imports, and therefore lead to demands for compensations. Such problems of sharing costs and benefits are common in any trade integration efforts.

Inadequate transport infrastructure is a problem waiting to be solved (cf. Chapter 1). The *ad valorem* incidence of shipping costs of intra-developing country trade is often considerably higher than for similar goods on the trade routes of the industrial countries. LDCs should accord high priority to the improvements that would need to be made to the present freight services, so that they are able to support enhanced intra-trade. The infrastructural bottlenecks and the skewed freight charges need to be streamlined.

Most, if not all, LDCs have their state trading organisations. Governments can step up intra-trade by means of these instruments. Upgrading marketing facilities would facilitate intra-trade. Because of the well developed marketing networks of the transnational corporations, LDCs find it easier to trade with the industrialised countries. At times they import products which are produced in LDCs through intermediaries based in the industrialised countries. International Trade in beverages is a case in point. Once the marketing institutions and facilities are developed in LDCs, such practices could be avoided.

The GSP and its Transitory Utility

Although Prebisch's plan had wisdom and resulted in some trade benefits to LDCs, a need for improvement in GSP has been felt for some time. For instance: the schemes (1) need to be simplified, (2) can be extended to more products, (3) the discriminatory treatment by several countries, which is presently in vogue, should be eschewed, (4) tariff reductions should be made binding, and (5) demands for reciprocity by the industrial countries should be discouraged. These issues can be addressed in the Uruguay Round. However, looked at against the background of the present macroeconomic climate, the industrial countries would find it difficult to concede on all of them.

Although, the GSP is welfare-expanding and has had some impact on the export earnings of a small number of LDCs, the system has managed to divert the attention of LDCs from full MFN trade liberalisation. It holds better prospects for trade expansion because:

(1)   neither all manufactured and semi-manufactured goods
       are covered by various GSP schemes;
(2)   nor are all the LDCs;
(3)   the tariff cuts are not binding under the GSP schemes;
(4)   many schemes enforce limits on the volume of trade
       which can benefit from reduced or zero-tariff rates;
(5)   the MFN tariff reductions provide more favourable
       access to world markets for unlimited trade volumes.

A full MFN trade liberalisation endeavour – which assumes
sufficient lifting of NTBs to allow the realisation of the full
potential of tariff liberalisation – would result in total direct
trade gains for the GSP beneficiaries of $17.8 billion. In the area
of clothing alone, it would lead to a potential trade expansion
of some $7.7 billion, which is greater than the value of the
present combined GSP schemes for all products.[22]
Substantial gains are also feasible in the area of textiles,
footwear, telecommunications equipment, furniture, travel
goods and toys. Some of the other products to benefit from
MFN liberalisation are preserved fruit, fresh and simply preserved fish, sugar and confectionery. MFN liberalisation would
be accompanied by some negative effects for LDCs; they have
been measured at $12.8 million in products like non-electrical
machinery, machines for special industries, photographic and
cinematographic supplies and medical equipment. However,
compared to the gains, the losses are minor.
LDCs must not look at the GSP benefits as a part of their
long-term trade strategy. As their capacity to make contributions or negotiated concessions improves with progressive
growth in their economies, they should try to move the international trade regime in the direction of MFN liberalisation. From
the perspective of long-term planning and investment, LDCs
need permanent and binding reductions in tariffs. The GSP
schemes do not offer this, while the MFN tariff reductions do.
They also offer an effective deterrent against other forms of
protection and quantitative restrictions.

Reforming the Safeguard Clause

The LDCs feel that the safeguard clause has been frequently
abused, which has had a deleterious effect on their exports. The

clause was originally designed as a defensive mechanism, but it is currently utilised as an offensive barrier to trade. It was meant to provide a temporary relief,[23] and the time to make the necessary structural adjustments in the economy. Instead it is observed that a great many times it facilitates the perpetuation of inefficient industries that lost their comparative advantage a long while ago. So-called temporary protection measures are often never repealed and tend to become permanent. The safeguard action against LDCs in the industrial countries would continue because of the continually changing comparative advantage. Its application is likely to keep moving from one successful LDC to another and from sector to sector. The GATT, therefore, needs a reformed and strengthened safeguard code, which should allow temporary protection in the industrial countries for the purpose of encouraging structural adjustment, and curb its current abuse. The issue was addressed in the Tokyo Round, but much to the chagrin of the LDCs, no agreement was reached.

Greenaway contends that if the importing countries were encouraged to use Article XIX more whenever the 'threat of injury' or 'serious injury' arises, there would be reduced incentive to circumvent it and seek recourse to NTBs. It would, undoubtedly, be beneficial because the protective measures thus taken would be 'official' and, therefore, less disruptive of the international trading order.[24] When the action is taken in an 'official' manner, it is known which countries are taking what measures in which product lines; it is not hidden and its economic consequences can be monitored.

That the MFN requirement should be dropped in order to encourage the widespread 'official' use of Article XIX, seems the most important reform to many industrial countries. It is based on the argument that the adjustment difficulties in the industrial country markets are invariably created by exports from the individual NICs; therefore, it is reasonable to take discriminatory measures against them. The justification of the industrial countries is: why should other countries be penalised by emergency action when they are not the sources of 'serious injury' to the importers? However, the developing countries, in particular the NICs, are sceptical of such a proposal. Although many LDCs have welcomed the idea of a reformed safeguard clause, they feel that if the discriminatory action was legalised they would be left in a highly exposed position. There is also an apprehension among LDCs that the 'threat of serious injury' could be somewhat loosely interpreted by the industrialised countries, and that controls could be imposed in product lines where comparative advantage is potential rather than real. Also, going by their MFA experiences, LDCs feel that selectivity will in fact be a license for discrimination.

For many there is a psychological barrier associated with dropping the MFN principle because it was the basic premise that was instrumental in the success of postwar trade liberalisation. Compromising the MFN smacks of either complete disintegration of the GATT framework, or its fragmentation into two sets of rules, one for the developed and the other for the developing countries. Once discrimination in international trade becomes acceptable, the general level of protection cannot but rise. The GATT considers non-discrimination a *conditio sine qua non*, a necessary and sufficient system-forming condition.[25] There is no way of maintaining an orderly and predictable international trading system without the MFN commitment.

A secondary deleterious effect of dropping the non-discrimination condition is also possible, that is, once an industrial country takes discriminatory action against an LDC, the latter is likely to intensify its exporting effort in the other industrial countries. This increases the pressure on the more exposed industrial countries, which are tempted to take discriminatory action, and a cycle is gradually established. There is evidence of this kind of ricocheting process in the multifibre arrangement. The MFN basis of Article XIX, therefore, should not be compromised and restraints should be non-discriminatory.

Perhaps the most cogent argument against selectivity is that Article XIX is not a punishment for the offending exporter, but an admission that the protected industry is no longer competitive. Since a non-discriminatory safeguard action affects all suppliers, actual and potential, they have a strong common interest in the early removal of the restrictions. This concentrates the pressure for adjustment where it ought to be – on the protecting country and the protecting industry.[26] This tangle has attracted a good deal of scholarly attention. One proposal to overcome the shortcomings of Article XIX was as follows:

countries contemplating emergency action can be permitted, under compelling circumstances, to take any discriminatory action 'officially'. However, there would be a *quid pro quo*, the country would accept a certain discipline. First, the discriminatory action would only be approved for a finite period and, secondly, the measures would be regressive over this period. For instance, if a discriminatory QR is imposed for five years, there might be zero growth of imports in year one, say, 5 per cent in year two, 10 per cent in year three and so on, until at the end of the fifth year all restrictions would be removed.[27]

Another way of ensuring the fair use of Article XIX is tight multilateral surveillance and control of all restrictive actions, except those taken under other GATT provisions. To this end, a GATT surveillance committee has been variously suggested. The reformed Article XIX should also involve the payment of compensation – as retaliation is not always possible for LDCs – to the affected exporters.

Ideally, it would be desirable for the industrial countries to eschew additional VERs, orderly marketing arrangements (OMAs), industry-to-industry restraint agreements and other kinds of NTBs in the future. It would also be desirable to have all the safeguard clause protection in the form of tariffs rather than QRs, and to have the proceeds earmarked for use in the adjustment process. This would also make the cost of protection visible. All safeguard measures should be transparent, with complete information provided to all who may possibly need it.

The interpretation of Article XIX could be improved by defining 'serious injury' more clearly and giving it an economic content. The protecting country should be made to see the clear economy-wide implications of the 'serious injury'. Many a time the 'serious injury' may not appear to be an injury at all. An OECD study provided insights into why the economy-wide costs and benefits of protection to industry are short-changed in decision-making. It is because the spread of protection in the economy and the perception of its negative ramification – causing a deleterious effect on the world economy – depends on three factors: (1) the costs and benefits of trade for domestic political actors; (2) these actors' access to and control over the process of government; and (3) the extent to which international commitments and obligations to trade policy are viewed as binding by national governments.[28] The political actors, whose time horizon, and so vision, is limited, become more important in taking economic decisions and cause economy-wide confusion.

A 'sunset clause' should be built automatically into all safeguard arrangements. If no time limit is applied to import restraints and an industry continues to be protected and subsidised after its loss of comparative advantage, the income of the factors of production in this industry would undoubtedly be maintained. But subsidising the factors to stay in this industry would discourage the much-needed structural adjustment, and there would be a long-term efficiency loss. This would have welfare-contracting implications for the protecting economy. A more prudent policy might be to subsidise the factors on condition that they move out. This is adjustment assistance, and means that the factors are not subsidised if they do not move.[29] This works as an incentive to structural adjustment.

The Services Sector

It is difficult to justify leaving an area as large and significant as trade in services outside an established international framework of norms. In order to discourage anarchy in trade in services, it would be desirable to have a mutually agreed set of trade regulations by the end of the 1980s It may well be that it is only possible to frame a very general code, but even that would be meaningful in retarding – if not arresting – the *ad hocism* and rampant growth of barriers to trade in services. Secondly, the general code would in time become a basis for subsequent detailed negotiations, and the development of a refined code. Despite the initial dissension, trade in services is being taken up for discussion – albeit on 'a parallel track' – during the Uruguay Round.

Some services may be protected on infant-industry grounds – as can trade in some goods – but if protection becomes more extensive and encompasses costly and poor quality indigenously-provided services, economic efficiency suffers, leading to welfare losses. The export sector *inter alia* becomes handicapped, because it utilises services upstream or downstream or both. Conceptually, the trade in services is not different from that in goods. At the end of the day, why does one buy a good? Because it provides some services. Therefore, it would be ideal to include services in the GATT charter, and to change it merely by adding 'and services' wherever the expression 'goods' occurs.

Access at a reasonable cost to quality services can make the difference between success or failure in export performance. If the LDCs' liberalised and more efficient and less expensive services become available to their economies, it would help them in their export endeavours, by lowering their costs. The developing countries should not lose sight of the fact that a great number of traded services are intermediates and influence the final product. Successful economies, like the East Asian NICs, ensure that internationally traded intermediate goods are available to domestic producers at world prices. Identical logic applies to internationally traded intermediate services as well. Second, it would encourage the multinational corporations to move away from goods to producing and providing services in LDCs. Third, if the industrial countries can sell more services, they may be more willing to lower protective barriers in sectors of interest to LDCs. A key issue in this context would be 'the right to establish' affiliates or branches in the importing country, and once they are established, it will have to be ensured that they receive non-discriminatory national treatment. The phrase 'right to establish' conceals a continuum of factor mobility phenomena which embraces both capital and mobility. It can cover the right of a Swiss bank to move to Senegal and set up a branch, implying foreign investment and the right to employ foreign personnel locally. Suggestions have been made to provide for the setting up of branch offices, and the right to employ foreign personnel. However, several countries have found these policy measures difficult to comply with and expressed reservations. The negotiations in this regard should make some headway in this direction.

The Group of Ten (cf. Chapter 3) was averse to trade liberalisation in services because they postulated that LDCs could not compete with industrialised countries in this sector. However, it would be wrong to suggest that LDCs cannot find traded services that can be exported successfully, or that they do not have a comparative advantage in services. Presently the services sector exports of LDCs are not negligible and seem to reflect earnings not only from tourism and transport but also from 'other private services', which include professional, design, construction and related services. Sapier (1985) calculated the dimensions of this trade for 1980, as follows:

(In billions of $)

	Industrialised-country exports to LDCs	LDCs' exports to industrialised countries
Services trade, of which:	72	30
Transport	35	10
Travel	14	12
Other private services	23	8

SOURCE   Sapir, A., 'North-South Issues in Trade in Services', *The World Economy*, March 1985, pp. 27–41, Table 2.

Also, the GATT data in Table 5.4 show that, taken as a fraction of total exports, the services exports of several LDCs are higher than those of several industrialised countries.

The East Asian NICs have managed to become successful traders in services. The US dominance of the international construction industry has been brought down by the middle-income LDCs. Also, in the more complex field of international design, a sizeable share of contracts are being awarded to firms from Brazil, India, Korea, Lebanon and Taiwan. Not only the NICs, but other middle-income LDCs have skills to develop an export edge not only in computer software, but also in an increasing range of computer services, referred to as 'on-the-line' services. Thus, the apprehension of the LDCs about not having comparative advantage in services is grossly exaggerated.

Strengthening the GATT

To stem the erosion and restore credibility in the system, the GATT as an institution needs to be strengthened. Its Secretariat should be enlarged and given initiatory powers to monitor

Table 5.4 SHARE OF SERVICES IN TOTAL EXPORTS
(percentage share in 1980)

30 to 40		41 to 48		51 to 96	
Belgium–Luxembourg	38	Antigua and Barbuda	44	Bahamas	83
Colombia	32	Austria	45	Barbados	68
Denmark	31	Egypt	41	Cyprus	56
Dominica	39	Fiji	43	Greece	51
France	37	Israel	41	Grenada	58
Haiti	30	Paraguay	42	Jordan	66
India	33	Senegal	46	Maldives	80
Jamaica	32	St Lucia	48	Malta	57
Kenya	39	St Vincent	47	Nepal	62
Mexico	35	Western Samoa	41	Panama	71
Norway	34			Lesotho	83
Portugal	33			Seychelles	94
Somalia	35			Tonga	57
Spain	39			Yemen Arab Rep.	96
Sudan	33			Yeman, People's Dom.	
Switzerland	30			Rep. of	66
Tunisia	40				
United Kingdom	34				
United States	35				
Uruguay	34				
Yugoslavia	34				

NB   Including factor income receipts.
SOURCE   *International Trade 85–86* (Geneva, GATT, 1986) Table A–39.

compliance of the Contracting Parties with their obligations under the GATT. A strong GATT can play a more independent role in underpinning the international trade system. It should be made into a full-fledged international institution like the World Bank and the International Monetary Fund.

The strengthening process should be so devised as to make the international trade regime transparent, liberal, stable and based on market-conforming instruments. A piecemeal approach, to this end, is likely to be inadequate. Also, an approach that does not involve all the Contracting Parties is unlikely to go far enough and invigorate the multilateral trade regime. For this purpose, the recommendations of a plan called GATT Plus' are being recalled by scholars.[30] It was put forward in a report of the Atlantic Council and elaborated specific proposals for a tighter and more comprehensive agreement than that embodied in the present GATT. The basic guiding principles are: first, that no country would submit to a significantly greater degree of discipline if it were painful to its domestic economy; and no country would significantly liberalise its trade barriers unless other countries also accepted corresponding changes in their trade policies. The improved trading order should ensure that no country substitutes another trade barrier for the one that has been dismantled in keeping with a specific code. For these reasons, the code that is intended to tighten the GATT discipline must be negotiated and adhered to as a 'package', as was the case with the GATT itself. Second, it must be understood that countries will not continue to accept that those who do not themselves abide by the disciplines of the multilateral trading system should have a say in the administration of the agreed code. Third, the agreement must be open, that is, countries willing to abide by the code can join in. The planners of a reinvigorating scheme should bear this philosophy in mind when embarking on devising the nuts and bolts of the proposal.

Strengthening the GATT would have two dimensions: first, GATT would be strong if the Contracting Parties could be coaxed into adhering to the GATT regulations and processes, rather than adopting *ad hoc* policy measures and bypassing the GATT code. Second, institutional changes in the GATT and the enlargement of its role can make it more efficient and effective. For instance, the GATT can play a more meaningful role in monitoring national and international trade policies and promoting transparency in trade-related measures. Departures from acceptable norms of behaviour should be reviewed periodically by the Secretariat and be tied to time schedules.

The curbs on the NTBs should be developed rapidly through a growing body of case laws and implemented faithfully under the GATT auspices. An eminently feasible measure to strengthen the GATT would be to give it a mandate to identify and publicise the existing trade barriers. A GATT subcommittee should be established to provide annual reviews of protection in all the major areas like agriculture, industrial safeguards, high technology goods, and special regimes like textiles and apparel and services.[31] This subcommittee should request formal statements from national governments and the trading blocs like the

EEC and EETA, on the rationale for protection, plan steps to reduce it, and determine the time schedule and the domestic adjustment measures. At present there are no regular analytical and evaluative reviews of a member country's trade policies. This could be remedied by an effective trade policy surveillance mediation scheme. The GATT should send regular reviewing teams to perhaps the 30 largest trading nations, while the smaller trading countries should be looked at occasionally. The objective is to assess the cost of protectionist measures and to notify it to the protecting country with suggestions for alternatives.

The Secretariat should mediate in disputes at an early stage and the judgement should be speeded up. The dispute panel rulings, which hitherto have not been binding, should be made so. The complained-against countries should not be given a veto to block adverse rulings. The disputes of the large trading powers like the EEC, the United States, Japan and Canada, must not be settled outside the GATT, on an *ad hoc* basis, which is commonly done. They should instead be channelled through the appropriate codes and articles of the GATT. The demonstrated ability to resolve conflicts among major traders through its codes and committees would strengthen the GATT and create confidence in the system of GATT-supported free trade. At present the GATT charter does provide for retaliation by the complaining countries, but this measure is of little use for LDCs, because of their limited trading muscle.

The current practice of appointing the dispute settlement panels from the officials representing the Contracting Parties has been widely criticised,[32] and scepticism about their objectivity has been in the air for a while. The decision-making process would improve if a permanent roster of experts, who are not currently representing any government, were maintained. The GATT Secretariat should also adopt the practice of initiating inquiries of its own against practices that appear to it to be questionable.

Unilateral action on the domestic trade policy front by the Contracting Parties could be an important element of a strengthened plan. This would have two objectives: (1) introducing economic rationality into the protection-related discussions; and (2) making the process of protection-granting transparent. The reforming Contracting Parties should insist on the more transparent forms of protection, like tariffs, auctioned quotas or subsidies. These measures give a clear economy-wide picture of the costs and benefits of protection. It is necessary for public education, so that the political decision-making process is not able to short-change them and that mercantilist fallacies be laid to rest. Wolf proposes two ways for achieving these objectives.[33] The first proposal is legal and comprises a non-discriminatory treaty which would make various covert administrative measures, like VERs, illegal. The concept of non-discrimination should be so interpreted that the only permissible quantitative restrictions are auctioned quotas. The second approach is technocratic and focuses on the economic content of protection-granting procedures. The economy-wide costs and benefits of any proposed protectionist policy measure should be publicly evaluated. A case in point is the current debate in the United States on the VERs imposed on Japanese car exports.

6 The Uruguay Round of Multilateral Trade Negotiations

1 THE INITIATION OF THE MOVEMENT

To complete the unfinished business of the Tokyo Round and to untangle the complexities spawned by neo-protectionism, the United States initiated an eighth round of multilateral trade negotiations (MTNs) at the 1982 GATT ministerial session; this was in the belief that only a fresh round of the MTN would be able to stall the tide of new protectionism and bring about a roll-back of trade-distorting measures. The GATT ministerial session established a working programme covering a wide range of issues for possible negotiation in a new round; a modest amount of technical and preparatory work was also done in terms of delineating the substance of a new round. The main issues that need to be addressed are reasonably clear.

The Uruguay Round offers a unique opportunity to provide the international community with a trading system that can function effectively for the rest of the century and beyond. The decision to launch the round demonstrates, *inter alia*, the significance that countries attach to strengthening the multilateral framework for guiding national trade policy-making.

For the sake of the congresses and parliaments which react to domestic sectoral pressures for protection, it is worth starting a fresh round of MTNs. It creates a counter-pressure that should keep the balance in favour of free trade. The lobbying and pressures for protection are usually far greater than those for free trade because typically the benefits of protection accrue to a few – namely the producers – while the costs are spread thinly over the consumers and the government. The ongoing negotiations help keep the protectionists – lobbyists and legislators – in check by invoking the possibility of upsetting the delicately poised multilateral talks.

The preparations and negotiations for the Punta del Este Declaration,[1] indicated the areas of agreement and discord among the Contracting Parties. The road to Punta del Este was hard and thorny, and despite wide ranging agreements, the underlying differences in positions were substantial regarding both the substantive issues to be negotiated and the modalities to be adopted during the negotiations. A broadly balanced set of commitments by developed and developing countries is necessary for achieving meaningful results. Following the creation of a Trade Negotiation Committee (TNC), which is responsible for the negotiations, a broad outline of the negotiating structure has been agreed. The Committee has two main negotiating groups – one on goods, and the other on services – reporting to it. The negotiations on trade in services will not be considered as GATT negotiations, but will form part of the Uruguay Round. Although negotiations on goods and services fall within the overview of the TNC, a clear distinction has been drawn between them. In addition, there are several subsidiary negotiating groups. However, work needs to be done about how the negotiations are to be undertaken, so that the results achieved are up to expectations. This preparation is important from the perspective of the LDCs because the negotiations held during the previous GATT rounds left them disgruntled. They voiced their disaffection in no uncertain terms after the Tokyo Round. Also, a good deal of rancour was subsequently created between the developed and developing countries during the 1982 GATT ministerial session.

As noted, the Group of Ten Countries showed little enthusiasm for the Uruguay Round. Brazil and India, the two most active LDC participants in the Tokyo Round, were the most vociferous opponents of launching the new round. They had two principal objections: (1) they doubted the ability and willingness of the industrial countries to commit themselves to significant trade liberalisation; and (2) trade in services, which was to be a high point of the negotiations, worried them partly because of strong domestic opposition, and partly because they postulated that the industrialised countries, in particular the United States and the EEC, were disposed to ask for a *quid pro quo*. The Group of Ten LDCs believed that the industrialised countries would pressure the developing countries to open their markets for trade in services in return for an access to their markets in goods. They preferred any discussion on services to be handled in the UNCTAD framework.

The agenda for the Uruguay Round is broadly in keeping with the aspirations of the LDCs, for the list of items to be negotiated includes tariffs, NTBs, safeguard mechanisms, trade in tropical products and those based on natural resources. The round offers an opportunity to achieve progress in several areas of vital importance to LDCs. For instance, they have been looking for improvements in a number of main articles of the GATT, notably in issues related to surveillance and dispute settlement. The LDCs can also utilise this opportunity to push for the domestic processing of their exports. The multifibre arrangement, although included, is hedged in such diplomatic language that little improvement can be expected in it. The General Principles Governing Negotiations, in their Section B-IV and B-V, reflect the desire of the LDCs to retain their 'special and differential status', and provide for more favourable treatment of LDCs. These sections also admit that the industrial countries will not expect 'reciprocity' for concessions to LDCs. Section B-VI reiterates the GATT's usual formula for recognising the graduation principle. Section B-VII promises special attention to the least-developed countries and to the expansion of their trading opportunities.[2] The GATT is of the view that a broadly based and widely supported round can recommence the movement towards trade liberalisation and help LDCs' interests.

There are several areas of special significance to LDCs. For instance, they have been concerned about trade in tropical products, which is obstructed by tariffs as well as by NTBs. Some progress in liberalising trade in tropical products has taken place since 1982; the current round should reflect the concern of the LDCs and attempt to broaden the range of tropical products brought under free trade. A related area of concern is the trade in natural resources products, notably fisheries and timber products. These products already face the problems of an unstable market, exacerbated by heightened protectionism. Besides, there is the wider question of the treatment of agricultural trade relevant to many LDCs. The current round offers possibilities of stopping the rampant bilateralism in agricultural trade, and dealing with issues like export subsidisation and domestic trade distortion measures.

Reform proposals have been prepared by the Cairns group, regarding trade and export subsidies, QRs and other restrictions. An agreement is sought on the management and disposal of surpluses. These ideas are to be developed with the back-up of econometric models and studies, and discussed in the Uruguay Round.

It is difficult to see how deliberations in the current round would achieve substantive and real movement towards a sound and rational trading system whose premise is free trade. The experiences of the Tokyo Round show a single set of negotiations achieves limited results – be it noted that in the current round a larger number of countries are seeking effective participation. A phased approach to negotiations would, indeed, be more functional. It is apparent that not all issues are of equal importance to all countries, some are more important to most than are others. Equally, some issues are much nearer to resolution than others. The phased approach, would tackle the issues in stages. These stages could be uneven in themselves but could take into account the interests of all the participating country groups. Eventually all issues would be incorporated into the rolling negotiations. The resolutions of the tangles would be approached in a pragmatic manner, providing for different approaches and timings.[3] This is known as the rolling or on-going negotiation process.

2   THE PARTICIPATION OF THE DEVELOPING COUNTRIES

Several LDCs presently participate in a big way in international trade. Many of the major participants have been reeling under an oppressive burden of debt and have, therefore, cut down on their imports, either voluntarily or as a part of their structural adjustment programmes. Several of these LDC participants are in the export of manufactures in a big way; in this regard Taiwan's performance is at its peak. The major trading LDCs, with and without debt burdens, are as shown in Table 6.1:

Table 6.1 EXPORTS AND IMPORTS OF MAJOR TRADING
LDCs (in billions of $)

	1985 Exports	1985 Imports	Exports of Manufactures		
			1979–81	1984–86	Annual Percentage Change between 1979–81 and 1984–86
	1	2	3	4	5
The heavily indebted LDCs					
1. Argentina	8,396	3,814	1.8	1.5	−3.5
2. Brazil	25,639	14,346	7.4	14.8	15.0
3. Colombia	3,462	4,498	0.7	0.6	−3.0
4. Indonesia	21,902	13,882	0.5	2.3	35.5
5. Mexico	22,108	13,993	4.3	10.1	18.5
6. The Philippines	4,607	5,459	2.0	2.5	5.0
The creditworthy LDCs					
1. Algeria	12,795	9,061	NA	NA	NA
2. China	27,327	42,526	NA	NA	NA
3. Egypt	3,714	9,961	NA	NA	NA
4. Hong Kong	30,184	29,705	12.5	17.2	6.5
5. India	7,915	14,608	4.4	4.7	1.5
6. Malaysia	15,442	12,302	2.2	4.2	15.2
7. Singapore	22,812	26,285	8.5	12.4	8.0
8. South Korea	29,566	31,129	16.0	28.7	12.5
9. Taiwan	NA	NA	17.1	30.5	12.5

SOURCE   Columns (1) and (2), *International Financial Statistics*
(Washington, DC: IMF, 1986).
Columns (3), (4) and (5) *International Trade 1986/87* (Geneva:
GATT, 1987).

From the new Round of MTN, the creditworthy LDCs, in particular the NICs, stand to gain the most. They also have the most to lose if the possibilities for export expansion are foreclosed. The sensitivity of the NICs to protection cannot be exaggerated. Protectionism against them did exist in the 1970s also, but it did not cripple them. They were able to upgrade their products and maintain a competitive edge in international markets. They used other devices to increase revenue on a stagnant or declining volume of trade.[4] However, the trade barriers they are presently facing could have a highly deleterious effect on their economies. There is a possibility of numerous salutary effects to these LDCs in an improved safeguard system and dismantling of QRs. These two measures would discernibly improve the access of the LDCs to the industrial country markets.

The NICs should play a more active role in the current round. Notwithstanding the fact that the non-reciprocity prerogative has been granted to them, from the current round on the large trading creditworthy LDCs, particularly the NICs, can endeavour to become full participants in negotiations. The GATT should explore the possibility of getting the high-income LDCs to accept reciprocity in trade negotiations. Now that their exports have grown, it is difficult to argue about their infancy without creating pressures on the grounds of unfair competition. Their self-interest lies in paying in concessions to the industrialised countries for the ones received from them. At this point, the NICs are better placed to play this game of give and take than the other LDCs. The level of participation can be determined on the basis of the balance of payments situation of the NIC in question. A beginning in this regard can be the lowering of absurdly high tariffs, say, those which are as high as 100 per cent and above. The second measure which is immediately applicable is either converting all QRs into auctioned quotas or into tariffs. The latter is preferable to the former. Further, the NICs can extensively bind tariffs and withdraw the regulations regarding countertrade requirements. They should also graduate from the special provisions of Part IV of the GATT and eschew the 'special and differential' status accorded to LDCs, as well as the GSP benefits. It is time they charted a reasonably specific programme for fully integrating their trade regimes into the GATT system. To be sure, such concessions would initially prove costly and painful, and may entail political costs. But this discipline will ensure the alignment of industries and the price structure in these countries to international markets. This kind of improvement in the domestic sector would have as much growth-promoting effect as better market access in the industrial countries. Up to this point LDCs have underestimated the potential benefits of negotiating for reciprocal reduction of trade barriers in the multilateral trade negotiations. Accepting reciprocity and assuming greater GATT obligations would help integrate them into the international trading system.

One important reason for the recent spate of NTBs in the industrial market economies is that, on the one hand, the LDCs enjoyed their 'special and differential' status, and on the other hand, the NICs began to outcompete the industrial countries in several product lines. When the economic crunch came and the protectionist lobbies become aggressive, the industrial countries accused the NICs of unfair trading and activated a variety of NTBs. The acceptance of reciprocity by the NICs would take the edge off such an accusation and relax the pressure exerted by the protectionist lobbies, eventually resulting in dismantling of the NTBs and streamlining of the international trade structure.

To sum up, the *raison d'être* of the Uruguay Round is to arrest creeping protectionism and bring about the liberalisation and expansion of the system making it responsive to changes in international competitiveness – all for the fuller and more efficient use of the world's resources. Implicit in these goals are the following supporting objectives: (1) to circumscribe the use of non-tariff barriers; (2) to ensure that the developing countries, while receiving some special treatment, participate in the negotiations and the more advanced ones assume responsibility for their GATT obligations; (3) to broaden and extend the coverage of GATT, particularly to services and agricultural products; and (4) to restore respect for the GATT system.[5]

3   THE ROAD TO WISDOM

The road to wisdom must have several roadside stations. Any substantive movement towards liberal trade has to involve several strategic steps, which would make the national economies more efficient and buttress their capacity for economic growth. In what follows I discuss the principal steps to be taken during the Uruguay Round. Some of these issues were unsuccessfully addressed during the Tokyo Round; this is another opportunity to resolve them. Hufbauer and Schott sequentially enumerate[6] the most significant of these issues.

The Standstill With a Difference

The industrialised countries presently have a substantial proportion of their trade protected in particular by NTBs. In the current round, they can commit to a standstill on new restrictions. In fact, such a condition should be applied to the trade of all the Contracting Parties without exception. The related agreement would discourage ingenious new trade barriers that contravene the spirit, and barely observe the letter, of the GATT charter. Reference is being made to the tailored standards for telecommunications equipment in the EEC, somewhat unrealistic safety and aesthetic standards for car imports in Japan, and the like. In some cases, these restrictions have been created as bargaining chips for the future negotiations.

The proposed standstill would be closely monitored and enforced. The GATT Secretariat would have a 'Standstill Panel' and the Contracting Parties would keep it posted regarding violations. In addition, the GATT Secretariat would do its own monitoring of infringements. The panel should also monitor all the countertrade requirements on import transactions valued over, say $10 million for the industrial economics, and, say, $5 million for the developing ones. Since the GATT framework does not cover trade in services, the Standstill Panel would not cover it either. In addition, a services standstill should be developed during the current round.

The Rollback

As a precondition to the new round, LDCs sought an agreement on 'rollback' and on the elimination of the 'grey area' measures. They deemed this necessary, because in the past they have had far too many experiences of evasion of commitments made by the industrialised countries. This elegant and simple proposal encountered considerable opposition. Many industrial countries likened it to the actual negotiations in various sectors, and found it unworkable and unacceptable. Instead, the alternatives they suggested were: (1) eliminating the 'grey area' measures, in a phased manner, in sectors where they are concentrated most; and (2) making rollback a major element of the negotiating framework. The large traders, who are the main users of the 'grey area' measures, give an impression of wanting to legitimise such measures. Therefore, they tried to circumscribe it by wording it in such a manner as to weaken the commitment. Such clever word play should be avoided, because ultimately it proves counterproductive and undermines the whole purpose of having a round of multilateral trade negotiations.

Although the concept of 'rollback' has been included in the Punta del Este Declaration, it incorporates two elements which dilute it: first the proposal for consultations could delay agreements on the implementation process; and second, the proposal that rollback should take into account multilateral agreements suggests that it might not become operative until the Uruguay Round negotiations are completed. Moreover, the Declaration has little in the name of specific commitment to 'rollback'. There is no mention of time-frames or schedules, which may become a real liability for trade in textiles and apparel, and in agriculture. The current Round should ensure adherence to rollback by way of close multilateral or GATT surveillance.[7]

The Expansion of the Scope of the GATT

Although textiles and apparel, and agriculture are technically under the aegis of the GATT, effectively they are not. Steel, dairy and pharmaceuticals are the other heavily protected sectors. As we have seen, except in minor ways, trade in services is also beyond the GATT discipline, so are the issues related to counter-trade and counterfeiting. As seen in Chapter 4, less than half of international trade abides by the GATT codes. The sectors listed above have the possibility of huge trade growth, both among LDCs and between developed and developing countries, and where potential efficiency gains from expanding trade are most conspicuous.

Expansion of the trade coverage of the GATT to include the aforenoted sectors should be, and is, one of the prime targets of the current round. Bringing textiles and agriculture under the GATT umbrella may be a time-consuming and frustrating exercise, but is not impossible. If tried in a phased manner, this goal is attainable.

Dismantling the QRs and NTBs

In the process of circumventing Article XIX, the industrial countries have applied QRs in a multiplicative manner. They have now come to be semi-permanent measures, and in many cases threaten to be permanent. Along the way, the safeguard principle has almost been forgotten. A specific objective should be to revise Article XIX so that such import restraints are applied in a non-discriminatory manner, and phased out according to the prescribed procedures.

In the current round the industrial countries should agree to replace the QRs by tariff measures. There are some signs of renewed interest in tariffs in the industrialised countries. They are being considered a means of replacing QRs. The rationale behind such a proposal is two-fold: first, it is assumed that it is not politically feasible to expect a prompt phase-out of QRs if there is nothing to replace them with. Second, tariffs have a number of advantages over QRs. For instance: (1) the discrimination involved in many QRs would be eliminated since tariffs are applied on a MFN basis; (2) the level of protection would be transparent; (3) tariffs are a more liberal device than QRs because the changes in international competitiveness can affect trade under tariffs but not trade subject to QRs; and (4) the reciprocal reductions in tariffs are easier to negotiate mutually than are reductions in QRs.

An alternative is to auction off the quotas and use the revenue for structural adjustment. This system, first, uses the price mechanism for allocating import rights, and, second the quota-rent would become a visible reminder of the presence of QRs in the system. The negotiators, however, must not be oblivious to the political pressures and the legitimate demands of failing industries. These have to be reconciled with the wider concepts of economic efficiency and the trade liberalisation objectives. A gradual, phased approach would be better than the brisk and choppy one.

The all pervading NTBs need to be attacked and demolished with the help of: (1) standstills on all new trade restrictions; (2) rollbacks of all QRs inconsistent with the provisions of the GATT; and (3) negotiated reductions and elimination of NTBs. Liberalising the NTBs is the greatest challenge for the Uruguay Round, because the current account imbalances in the world economy are large and the political economy of these measures is complex. The GATT system and its modes for eliminating NTBs are not always adequate. There is a problem of equivalence of various measures. If the reductions were carried out on the basis of strict reciprocity, some conversion factors would need to be worked out to reduce QRs. This apparently would make the procedure necessarily complex and difficult for the negotiators. That apart, there is the problem of illegal NTBs, that is, those introduced outside the GATT rules.[8] One proposal is that illegal NTBs could be eliminated in exchange for legal NTBs. Those who oppose it believe that such an exchange might establish a bad precedent for future trade negotiations. NTBs in agriculture pose a different problem from the rest of the NTBs. Their elimination would require international co-ordination of domestic policy. However, an internationally agreed limit can be imposed on the amount of farm output that could benefit from governmental support.

The equivalence issue can be settled by an agreement on a time limit for phasing out NTBs. Another useful measure is the growth rate in the market share of restricted imports. Secondly, the swapping of QRs with tariffs has been proposed; once this is achieved, the tariffs can then be gradually reduced. The traditional method of give-and-take can also be utilised for eliminating NTBs. Under GATT surveillance, the illegal NTBs can be dismantled. The VERs can be replaced by GATT-approved measures, or waivers under Article XXV may be requested.[9]

Promoting Fair Trade

The concept of fair trade is a fluid one. What is fair to one country or firm is unfair to another. Fairness, like truth, beauty and contact lenses, lies in the eyes of the beholder. Any sector of industry which loses market screams unfair competition. Three fairness issues have been in the forefront: (1) subsidies; (2) misuse of intellectual property; and (3) unbalanced concessions.

The simplest of these is subsidies. In the area of agricultural trade they have been a source of serious friction between the United States and the EEC. Subsidised export credits have been for some time – and continue to be – a source of friction among a number of industrialised and developing countries. Most firms find it difficult to compete against subsidised products; they feel that they are pitted against the national treasuries. This issue was addressed in the Tokyo Round but clever national governments successfully exploited the available loop- holes. Second, intellectual property, for instance, patented technology, design and copyrights are widely misused. Third, numerous examples of unbalanced concessions can be cited. The current round is an opportunity to strengthen the fabric of codes against these unfair trade practices.

The subsidy issue has caused a great deal of disaffection with the existing GATT regulations. The developed and developing countries both subsidise their industries for different sets of reasons. LDCs do so generally on infant-industry grounds, while many EEC countries do so because some of their tradi-tionally export-oriented industries have been losing their foreign market shares. Similarly, US industries benefit from the large defence and space expenditures of the government. All subsidising countries believe that theirs are the only justifiable reasons for using subsidies, while other countries' subsidies are aimed at causing injury to their domestic industries. To recon-cile them all, one has to distinguish between domestic subsidies of the beggar-thy-neighbour kind and those that can really be justified on structural adjustment grounds. Temporary and regressive subsidies could be permitted for export-oriented industries that have been seriously injured by competition in third markets. Those applied for infant-industry reasons are also justifiable from an economic viewpoint. Nevertheless, the permissible subsidies have to be temporary and regressive. Comprehensive subsidies negotiations are needed to reach a mutually acceptable agreement in this regard. Subsidies for shifting market shares must be outlawed.

The GATT charter contains several provisions relating to the use of subsidies, for instance, Articles VI, XVI and XXIII as modified in 1955, deal with these issues. These provisions were further elaborated during the Tokyo Round, the outcome was the Agreement on Interpretation and Application of Articles VI, XVI and XXIII, called the Subsidies Code, which became effective in January 1980. The GATT Articles and the Subsidies Code establish a concensual framework of rights and obliga-tions of Contracting Parties in relation to subsidies and counter-vailing duties. The Subsidies Code expands upon the existing

GATT provisions and also provides guidance on procedures for international dispute settlement. Article 14:2 of the Subsidies Code allows LDCs – though not unconditionally – to adopt any measures or policy to assist their industries, including those in the export sector. This assistance cannot continue for an indefinite period. According to the code, the subsidies have to be reduced or eliminated when the use of such export subsidies is inconsistent with its competitive and development needs. When such a commitment is made by an LDC, the Code guarantees that counter-measures other than countervailing duties against its exports shall not be authorised. Seemingly LDCs can use export subsidies, but they are not free from the risk of being countervailed, if in fact, their use of subsidies causes or threatens material injury to an importing country's industry. Thus, in reality the preferential treatment does not amount to much and the code is reduced to mere rhetoric.[10] This calls for a new multilateral negotiation on subsidy.

The Conditional MFN Principle

The MFN principle is regarded as the cornerstone of the GATT framework. Its merits are beyond doubt. It makes sound economic sense and is valuable politically. The issue in the current round is whether new obligations should be extended on an unconditional basis to all the Contracting Parties, or whether they should be granted on a conditional basis only to those countries that reciprocate, and make concessions in return.

The proponents of conditional MFN argue that the unconditional tariff-cutting approach of the first six rounds of the MTN was functional while the bulk of world trade was conducted among the United States, the EEC, Canada and Japan, and as long as the trading partners also traded substantial concessions with each other. The problem arose, however, when the number and participation of 'free riders' and 'foot draggers' became large. A 'free rider' is a small, usually developing country that offers no trade concessions, but by virtue of the MFN clause, enjoys the benefits of concessions made by other countries. An individual 'free rider' is not of notable significance, but several of them collectively do create a significant leakage when the trade benefits are extended on an unconditional MFN basis. With an increasing number of LDCs joining in the world trade, the number of 'free riders' has increased. On the other hand, a 'foot dragger' is a country which is such a large trader in a particular product line that no agreement can be reached without its participation in the multilateral negotiations. This role can be potentially played by the United States, Japan or the EEC in various product lines.

The countries falling in the above two categories can inhibit the granting of concessions in an unconditional MFN system, which would perpetuate the existing trade barriers. When countries act like 'free riders' and 'foot draggers' they become a strain on the GATT framework; in fact they have increasingly had a debilitating influence over the GATT system. In the Tokyo Round an irate United States insisted on adopting a conditional MFN position on issues like subsidies and government procurement. It is possible that the use of conditional MFN may widen. We return to the old recommendations. LDCs like Brazil, India and Korea are expected to trade some concessions with the Americans, Japanese and EEC if they want entry into their textiles, steel and sugar markets.

It has been argued (Cf. Chapter 4) that permitting conditional application of the MFN principle in safeguard cases is necessary if the GATT is to play a central role in maintaining an open trading framework.[11] Unequal treatment among countries already occurs under the GATT; customs unions and the GSP are cited as a reason why a shift to the selectivity principle in safeguard cases should not be regarded as too radical. The other side of the coin is that if the conditional MFN is adopted as a rule of the game, it would lead to increased discrimination and promote bilateralism, which would mean a reduction in world income, as the low cost producers are replaced by high-cost suppliers. Although it has not been given any thought as yet, the operation and management of a conditional MFN system would be an enormously cumbersome task. Moreover, it would lead to fragmentation and regionalisation of the world trading system. The result may well be a 'reciprocity club' in which only the members enjoy the cucumber sandwiches and cricket. This dichotomy would lead to a resurgence of the economic blocs that prevailed earlier in this century. In this scenario, the LDCs would be reduced to 'frozen little match girls, looking in on the festivities'.[12] This is the strongest argument against conditional MFN. The cornerstone of the GATT system, therefore, must not be disturbed.

Dispute Settlement Procedures

This was another issue which was addressed in the Tokyo Round. The procedures are widely believed to be slow and the GATT lacks clout in this regard. The reasons for the deficiency could be either (1) that the provisions to Articles XXII and XXIII are inadequate, or (2) that the Contracting Parties do not support the spirit and the letter of the provisions, or (3) a bit of both. Baldwin has alleged that the panels of experts appointed to render non-binding decisions in a dispute are influenced by political pressures from the disputants, especially the major trading powers.[13] Some countries have blocked the adoption of a panel's decision by the Contracting Parties when this decision was unfavourable to themselves. Even when a decision has been adopted by the other Contracting Parties, some countries have continued to ignore it.

The Tokyo Round debate focused on two main elements: (1) speeding-up the settlements, and (2) strengthening the whole process. The Contracting Parties were mainly concerned about the time taken in establishing the panel, and then in reporting to the Contracting Parties and eventually in taking action on the report by the Contracting Parties. The 1982 ministerial session did not propose a fundamental change but recognised the need for a more effective use of the existing mechanism. It included expediting the formation of panels as well as the conciliatory process. Subsequently, other proposals were made to facilitate the formation of panels and the completion of their work.

The Punta del Este Declaration text includes both improving the regulations of dispute settlement, and strengthening the compliance mechanism. The two measures could become the basis for invigorating the dispute settlement mechanism. What the round should aim at is: (1) an improved notification system; (2) more effective and swifter working procedures by panels; (3) more equitable treatment of LDCs; (4) increased and more effective surveillance by both the Secretariat and the Contracting Parties.[14]

Surveillance and Monitoring

An urgent need for improved surveillance and monitoring of commitments relating to standstills and rollbacks has increasingly been felt. Surveillance is also needed for the dispute settlement procedures. The Punta del Este Declaration does reflect these concerns of LDCs. Creation of a trade policy monitoring division in the GATT Secretariat is highly recommended. Improved surveillance within the GATT would also enhance the Contracting Parties' ability to monitor their trade policy. To this end, the role of the GATT Secretariat should be expanded to include the periodic review of the trade policy of the Contracting Parties and the international trading system.

The success, or otherwise, of the Uruguay Round would influence the *fin de siècle* scenario of international trade and economic growth. This round is considered the most significant since the inception of the GATT. Comprehensive negotiations leading to mutually acceptable agreements are necessary for revamping the entire liberal international trading order.

NOTES

1 The Contemporary Trade Scenario

1. The second wave of export pessimism was to sweep the international economic scene in the 1980s, when it was believed that although the markets existed, they would be shut off by rising protectionism.
2. Selowsky, M., 'Adjustment in the 1980s; An Overview of Issues', *Finance and Development*, June 1987, pp. 11–14.
3. International Monetary Fund, *Direction of Trade Statistics 1987*, Washington DC, 1987.
4. Larson, E. D., M. H. Ross and R. H. Williams, 'Beyond the Era of Materials', *Scientific American*, Vol. 254, June 1986, No. 6.
5. For a detailed discussion see UNCTAD, 'Impact of New and Emerging Technologies on Trade and Development', TD/B/C 6/136, August 1986.
6. We shall return to this in discussing the NICs because among the developing countries they dominate trade in manufactures.
7. *Economist*, Economic and Financial Indicators, 3 October, 1987, p. 115.
8. The General Agreement on Tariffs and Trade. *International Trade 1983–84*, and *1986–87*, Geneva, 1983 and 1988, Table 4.
9. Cf. Chapter 2.
10. Havrylyshyn, O. and M. Wolf, *Trade among Developing Countries: Theory, Policy Issues and Principal Trends*, Washington DC, World Bank Staff Working Paper No. 479, 1981. This is the most comprehensive, if somewhat dated, quantitative analysis on intra-LDCs trade. Their analysis was based on data for 1963 through 1977, for a sample of 33 LDCs, accounting for two-thirds of LDC exports.
11. Lall, S., 'South-South Economic Co-operation and Global Negotiations' in J. N. Bhagwati and J. G. Ruggie (eds.), *Power, Passions and Purpose* (Cambridge, Mass.: The MIT Press, 1984) pp. 287–322.
12. UNCTAD, *Statistical Note by the UNCTAD Secretariat*, TD/B/C 7/86, Geneva, 16 June, 1988.
13. Cizelje, B. and M. Fuks, 'Trade Among Developing Countries: Achievements and Potential' in Oli Havrylyshyn (ed.), *Exports of Developing Countries: How Direction Affects Performance* (Washington, DC: The World Bank, 1987) pp. 141–7.
14. UNCTAD (1988), op. cit.
15. Strant, A. M., *Structural Determinants of South-South Trade Expansion* (Cambridge, Mass.: Massachusetts Institute of Technology, February 1985, mimeographed).
16. Amsden, A. H., 'The Directionality of Trade: Historical Perspective and Overview' in Oli Havrylyshyn (ed.), *Exports of Developing Countries: How Direction Affects Performance* (Washington, DC: World Bank, 1987).

17. Maizels, A., *Industrial Growth and World Trade* (Cambridge: Cambridge University Press, 1963).
18. Yeats, A. J., 'A Comparative Analysis of Tariffs and Transport Costs on India's Exports', *The Journal of Development Studies*, No. 1, 1977, pp. 97–107.
19. Yeats, A. J., *Trade and Development Policy: Leading Issues for the 1980s* (London: Macmillan, 1983).
20. Lewis, W. A., 'The Slowing Down of the Engine of Growth', *The American Economic Review*, September 1980, pp. 555–64.
21. *GATT Press Release*, No. 1432, 29 February, 1988, p. 7.
22. *Economist*, 20 February, 1988, p. 24.
23. UNIDO, *World Industry since 1960s: Progress and Prospects* (New York: United Nations, 1979).
24. Chenery, H. B. and D. B. Keesing, *The Changing Composition of Developing Country Exports* (Washington, DC: World Bank Staff Working Paper No. 314, 1979).
25. Lorenz, D., 'New Situations Facing the NICs in East Asia', *Intereconomics*, November/December 1986, pp. 263–8.

2   The Link: Trade Policy and Economic Growth

1. Krueger, Ann O., 'Export Prospects and Economic Growth: India: A Comment', *The Economic Journal*, June 1961, pp. 436–42.
2. Cairncross, A., *Factors in Economic Development* (London: Allen & Unwin, 1962).
3. Riedel, J., *Myths and Reality of External Constraints on Development* (London: Gower for Trade Policy Research Centre, 1987) pp. 13–16.
4. Michalopoulos, C. and Keith Jay, *Growth of Exports and Income in the Developing World: A Neo-classical View*, AID Discussion Paper No. 28 (Washington, DC: Agency for International Development, 1973).
5. Michaely, M., 'Exports and Growth: An Empirical Investigation', *The Journal of Development Economies,* March 1977, pp. 49–53.
6. Krueger, A. O., *Foreign Trade Regimes and Economic Development: Liberalization Attempts and Consequences,* (New York: Colombia University Press for NBER, 1978: see Chapter 11 for details).
7. Balassa, Bela, 'Exports and Economic Growth: Further Evidence', *The Journal of Development Economists*, June 1978, pp. 181–9. See also Balassa, Bela, 'Export Incentives and Export Performance in Developing Countries: A Comparative Analysis', *Weltwirtschaftliches Archiv*, Band 114, 1978, No. 1, pp. 24–61.
8. Foder, G., 'On Exports and Economic Growth', *The Journal of Development Economics*, February/April 1983, pp. 59–74.
9. Chow, P. C. Y., 'Causality Between Export Growth and Industrial Development', *The Journal of Development Economics*, No. 26, 1987, pp. 55–63.
10. Balassa, Bela, *Exports, Policy Choice and Economic Growth in Developing Countries After the 1973 Oil Shock* (Washington, DC: World Bank DRD Paper No. 48, May 1983).

11. Balassa, Bela, 'Structural Adjustment Policy in Developing Countries: *World Development*, Vol. 10, No. 1, 1982.
12. Little, I. M. D., T. Scitovsky and M. Scott, *Industry and Trade in Some Developing Countries: A Comparative Study* (London: Oxford University Press, 1970).
13. Tsiang, S. C., 'Foreign Trade and Investment as a Booster for Take-Off: The Experience of Taiwan' in Vithoria Carbo, *et. al.* (ed.), *Export-Oriented Development Strategies* (Boulder, Col.: Westview Press, 1985).
14. Kim, K. S., 'Lessons from South Korea's Experience with Industrialization', in Vithorio Carbo, *et al.*, op. cit.
15. Lal, D. and S. Rajapatirana, 'Foreign Trade Regimes and Economic Growth in Developing Countries', *The World Bank Research Observer*, July 1987, pp. 172–89.
16. Greenaway, D. and C. H. Nam, 'Industrialisation and Macroeconomic Performance in Developing Countries under Alternative Trade Strategies', *Kyklos*, Vol. 41, 1988, Facs. 3, pp. 419–35.
17. Rhee, J. W., *Instruments For Export Policy and Administration*, World Bank Staff Working Paper, No. 725 (Washington, DC: World Bank, March 1985) pp. 8–9.
18. Ranis, G., 'Challenge and Opportunities Posed by Asia's Superexporters' in W. Baer and M. Gillis (eds), *Export Diversification and the New Protectionism* (Urbana: University of Illinois, 1981).
19. Little, I. M. D., *Economic Development: Theory, Policy and International Relations* (New York: Basic Books, 1982).
20. Diaz-Alejandro, C. F., 'Trade Policy and Economic Development' in P. B. Kenen (ed.), *International Trade and Finance* (Cambridge: Cambridge University Press, 1975).
21. Streeten, P., 'A Cool Look at Outward-Looking Strategies for Development', *World Economy*, September 1982, pp. 159–69.
22. Cline, W. R., 'Can the East Asian Model of Development Be Generalised?', *World Development*, Vol. 10, February 1982, pp. 81–90.
23. Harvylyshyn, O. and I. Alikhani, 'Is there cause for Export Optimism? An Enquiry into the Evidence of a Second-Generation Successful Exports', *Weltwirtschafts Archiv*, Vol. 118, 1982, pp. 651–62. See also Bhagwati, J. N., 'Export-Promoting Trade Strategy', *The World Bank Research Observer*, January 1988, pp. 27–57.
24. Bhagwati, J. N., 'Outward Orientation: Trade Issues', in Vittoria Corbo, M. Goldstein and M. Khan (eds), *Growth-Oriented Adjustment Programs* (Washington, DC: International Monetary Fund, 1987).
25. Ranis, G., 'Can the East Asian Model of Development Be Generalised? A Comment', *World Development*, Vol. 13, 1985, No. 4, pp. 543–5.
26. Hughes, H. and J. Waelbroeck, 'Can Developing Country Exports Keep Growing in the 1980s?', *The World Economy*, June 1981, pp. 127–47.
27. Havrylyshyn, O., *Penetrating the Fallacy of Export Composition: Or Hobson's Second Falsehood Revisited* (Washington, DC: World Bank, November 1986, mimeo).
28. Ibid., pp. 19–20.

3 Developing Countries in the Multilateral Trading System

1. *GATT Press communiqué* No. 1428, 20 January, 1988.
2. Finger, J. M., 'Trade Liberalization: A Public Choice Perspective', in Ryan Amacher, Gottfried Haberler and Thomas Willett (eds), *Challenge to A Liberal International Order* (Washington, DC: American Enterprise Institute, 1979).
3. Deepak, Lal, in his book 'Poverty of Development Economics' (London: Institute of Economic Affairs, 1983), launches an attack with devastating fire-power on the muddle-headed trade policies of the Government of India.
4. Bhagwati, J. N. and V. K. Ramaswami, 'Domestic Distortions and the Theory of Optimum Subsidy', *The Journal of Political Economy*, February 1963.
5. World Bank, *World Development Report 1987* (Washington, DC: 1987) p. 124.
6. National Bureau of Economic Research (NBER), 1975–76 (New York: Columbia University Press, Vol. I through Vol. IX, 1976, Vol. X and Vol. XI).
7. Organisation for Economic Co-operation and Development (OECD) (Oxford University Press, 1970, Vol. I through Vol. VI).
8. Tymowski, M. J., 'Trade Information System on Barriers to Trade Among Developing Countries: Methodological Considerations and Findings', in Oli Havrylyshyn (ed.), *Exports of Developing Countries: How Direction Affects Performance* (Washington, DC: The World Bank, 1987).
9. Anjaria, S. J., *et al.*, *Trade Policy Issues and Development* (Washington, DC: International Monetary Fund, Occasional Paper No. 38, July 1985).
10. General Agreement on Tariffs and Trade. *Report of the Tariffs Surveillance Body of the Textiles Committee*. COM/TEX/SB/984. (Geneva: GATT, October 1984).
11. Corden, W. M., *Protection and Liberalization: A Review of Analytical Issues* (Washington, DC: International Monetary Fund, Occasional Paper No. 54, August 1987).
12. Murray, T., *Trade Preferences for Developing Countries* (London: Macmillan, 1977).
13. Badgett, L. D., 'Preferential Tariff Reductions: The Philippine Response 1900–1940', *Journal of International Economies*, Vol. 8, 1978, No. 1, pp. 79–92.
14. Sawyer, W. C. and R. L. Sprinkle, 'Caribbean Basin Economic Recovery Act: Export Expansion Effects', *Journal of World Trade Law*, Vol. 18, 1984, No. 5, pp. 429–36.
15. Rousslang, D. and J. Lindsey, 'The Benefits of Caribbean Basin Countries from the U.S. CBI Tariff Elimination', *Journal of Policy Modeling*, Vol. 6, 1984, No. 4, pp. 513–30.
16. Pelzman, J. and G. K. Scheopfle, 'The Impact of the Caribbean Basin Economic Recovery Act on Caribbean Nation's Exports and Development', 1986, mimeo.

17. Ouattara, A. D., 'Trade Effects of the Association of African Countries With the European Economic Community', *International Monetary Fund Staff Papers*, Vol. 20, 1973, No. 2, pp. 499–543.
18. Ibid, chapter 2.
19. Sapir, A. and L. Lundberg, 'The US Generated Systems of Preferences and its Impact', in Robert E. Baldwin and Anne O. Krueger (eds), *American Trade Relations* (Chicago, Il.: University of Chicago Press, 1986).
20. World Bank, *Linkage Between Trade and Promotion of Development* (Washington, DC: 1986) pp. 29–30.
21. Ibid, p. 30. See also Baldwin, R. E. and T. Murray, 'MFN Tariff Reductions and Developing Country Trade Benefits Under the GSP', *The Economic Journal*, March 1977, pp. 30–46.
22. The US Congress, *Generalised System of Preferences* (Washington, DC: Subcommittee on International Trade, 1986) pp. 5–6.
23. Karsenty, G. and S. Laird, *The Generalised System of Preferences* (Geneva: UNCTAD Discussion Paper No. 18, 1986) Table A, p. 9.
24. Ibid. p. 15.
25. Organisation of Economic Co-operation and Development, *The Generalised System of Preferences: Review of the First Decade* (Paris: OECD, 1983).
26. Brown, D. K., 'Trade Preferences for Developing Countries: A Survey of Results', *The Journal of Development Studies*, April 1988, pp. 335–63.
27. Lande, S. and C. VanGrasstek, *Trade and Tariff Act of 1984* (Massachusetts: Lexington, 1986).
28. Cf. Chapter 4.
29. Kostecki, M., 'Export-restraint Arrangements and Trade Liberalization', *The World Economy*, December 1987, pp. 425–56.
30. Schumacher, D., 'Imports from Developing Countries: Reasons for Protection and Proposal for Liberalization', *Intereconomics*, November/December 1984, pp. 274–9.
31. Quoted in *Protection, Trade Restrictions and Structural Adjustment* (Geneva: UNCTAD, June 1983) pp. 11–14.
32. *Costs and Benefits of Protectionism* (Paris: OECD, 1985).
33. Whally, J., *Trade Liberalization Among Major World Trading Area* (Cambridge, MA.: MIT Press, 1985) Chapter II, Table 11.2.
34. Ibid.
35. UNCTAD, *Revitalizing Development, Growth and International Trade*, Geneva, July 1987, pp. 136–7.
36. *Problems of Protectionism and Structural Adjustment*, TD/B/1160 (Geneva: UNCTAD, April 1988).
37. Jung-ho, Yoo, *Free Trade Without Fair Trade is Unsustainable* (Seoul: Korean Development Institute, 1985).
38. *Economist*, 'Economic and Financial Indicators', 31 October, 1987, p. 96.
39. Riddle, D., *Service-led Growth* (New York: Praeger, 1986).
40. Nusbaumer, J., *The Service Economy: Lever to Growth* (Boston: Kluwer Academic Publications, 1987) pp. 99–101.

41. Sampson, G. P. and R. H. Snape, 'Identifying the Issues in Trade in Services', *The World Economy*, No. 8, 1985, pp. 171–81.
42. *Revitalising Development, Growth and International Trade* (New York: UNCTAD, 1987) pp. 162–3.

4 The Erosion of the GATT Framework

1. The International Trade Organisation (ITO) charter was not ratified because, as it was conceived, it had too many teeth for some of the participants at the conference. They saw in it a threat to their autonomy.
2. Even the toothless GATT can exert some subtle pressures effectively. For instance, pressures can come from the need to maintain negotiating credibility in the system.
3. Krueger, Anne O., and C. Michalopoulos, 'Developing Country Trade Policies and the International Economic System' in E. H. Preeg (ed.), *Hard Bargaining Ahead: US Trade Policy and Developing Countries* (New-Brunswick: Transaction Books, 1985) p. 45.
4. GATT, *Trade Policies for a Better Future* (Geneva: 1985). See also W. R. Cline (ed.), *Trade Policies in the 1980s* (Washington, DC: Institute for International Economics, 1983).
5. Wolf, M., 'Fiddling While the GATT Burns', *The World Economy*, March 1986, pp. 1–19.
6. *Trade and Development Report 1984*, Part II (Geneva: UNCTAD, 1984).
7. Cohen, S., 'Aspects of New Mercantilism: Barter, Countertrade, Buy-back and Offsets'. Paper presented at the conference on 'Security and National Prosperity in A Changing World Economy' organised by the Friedrick-Ebert-Stiftung, May 1985. Quoted by Larenz, D. in 'A GATT For the Mercantilists?' *Intereconomics*, Nov./Dec. 1985. See also *Economist*, 24 October, 1987.
8. Destler, I. M., *American Trade Policies: System Under Stress* (Washington, DC: Institute for International Economics, 1986) p. 47.
9. Anderson, K. and Y. Hayami, *The Political Economy of Agricultural Protection* (London: Allen & Unwin, 1986).
10. Valdes, A., 'Agriculture in the Uruguay Round: Interest of Developing Countries', *The World Bank Economic Review*, September 1987, pp. 571–93.
11. This is a group of countries that export agricultural products, and is composed of Argentina, Australia, Brazil, Canada, Chile, Colombia, Fiji, Hungary, Indonesia, Malaysia, the Philippines, New Zealand, Thailand and Uruguay.
12. *Financial Times*, 1 March, 1988, p. 6.
13. Das, Dilip K., 'Dismantling the Multifibre Arrangement?', *The Journal of World Trade Law*, January/February 1985, pp. 67–81.
14. Cable, V., 'Textiles and Clothing', in J. M. Finger and A. Olechowski (eds), *The Uruguay Round: A Handbook on the Multilateral Trade Negotiations* (Washington, DC: The World Bank, 1987).

15. *International Trade 1985/86* (Geneva: GATT, 1986).
16. GATT, *Basic Instruments and Selected Documents, Twenty-Six Supplement*, Geneva, March 1980, p. 203.
17. Article XIX, para 1 (b).
18. Article XIX, para 3.
19. Greenaway, D., *International Trade Policy: From Tariff to the New Protectionism* (London: Macmillan, 1983) pp. 214–15.

5 The Policy Blueprint

1. Haberler, G., 'Liberal and Illiberal Development Policy' in G. M. Meier (ed.), *Pioneer in Development* (New York: Oxford University Press, Second Series, 1987) pp. 80–1.
2. Lal, D., *The Poverty of Development Economies* (London: The Institute of Economic Affairs, 1984) p. 106.
3. Anjaria, S. J., *et al.*, *Trade Policy Issues and Developments* (Washington, DC: International Monetary Fund. Occasional Paper No. 38, July 1985).
4. Agarwala, R., *Price Distortion and Growth in Developing Countries* (Washington, DC: World Bank, Staff Working Paper No. 575, 1983) p. 13.
5. Cambridge Economic Policy Group, *Economic Policy Review* (Cambridge: Cambridge University Press, 1976).
6. Corden, W. M., *Protection, Growth and Trade: Essays in International Economics* (Oxford: Basil Blackwell, 1985).
7. This was a World Bank norm, mentioned in Agarwala (1983). Op. cit.
8. The World Bank, *World Development Report, 1987* (Washington, DC: Oxford University Press for the World Bank, June 1987) pp. 110–12.
9. Krueger (1978).
10. World Bank (1987), op. cit., p. 111.
11. *World Development Report, 1987* (Washington, DC: The World Bank, June 1987) pp. 82–94.
12. Krueger, Anne O., 'The Experience and Lessons of Asia's Super Exporters' in Vittorio Corbo, *et al.* (eds.), *Export Oriented Development Strategies* (Boulder: Westview Press, 1985) pp. 187–248.
13. Held in Belgrade, in June 1983.
14. Where the Uruguay Round of the MTN began in September 1986.
15. *Revitalizing Development, Growth and International Trade* (Geneva: UNCTAD, July 1987) p. 138.
16. *The World Bank, World Development Report, 1986* (New York: Oxford University Press, 1986) Table 6.5.
17. Cf. Chapter 3.
18. Krueger, Anne O. and C. Michalopoulos, 'Developing Countries, Trade Policies and International Economic Systems' in E. H. Preeg (ed.), *Hard Bargaining Ahead: US Trade Policy and Developing Countries* (New Brunswick: Transactions Books, 1985).
19. UNCTAD. *Ministerial Declaration on the Global System at Trade Preferences among Developing Countries* (9GSTP/L, 24), New Delhi, July 1985.

20. Erzan, R., Samuel Laird and Alexander Yeats, *On the Potential for Expanding South-South Trade Through the Extension of Mutual Preferences Among Developing Countries* (Geneva: UNCTAD Discussion Paper No. 16, 1986).
21. Ibid.
22. Karsenty, G. and S. Laird, *The Generalised System of Preferences: A Quantitative Assessment of the Direct Trade Effects and of Policy Options* (Geneva: UNCTAD Discussion Paper No. 18, 1986).
23. Article XIX: 1 (A) reads ' . . . for such time as may be necessary to prevent or remedy such injury . . . '.
24. Greenaway, D., *International Trade Policy: From Tariffs To The New Protectionism* (London: Macmillan, 1983) pp. 215–17.
25. *International Trade 1983/84* (Geneva: GATT, 1984) p. 20.
26. *Trade Policies for a Better Future: Proposals for Action* (Geneva: GATT, 1985) p. 43.
27. Tumlir, J., 'Emergency Protection Against Sharp Increases in Imports', in H. Corbet and R. Vackson (eds), *Effective Tariff Protection* (London: Croom Helm, 1971).
28. *Economic Relations Between Developed and Developing Countries: Situation and Prospects* (Paris: OECD, 1986) pp. 19–20.
29. See, for a detailed treatment, 'Policies Towards Market Disturbances' by W. Max Corden in *Issues in World Trade Policy*, edited by H. R. Snape (London: Macmillan, 1986).
30. *GATT Plus: A Proposal for Trade Reform* (Washington, DC: The Atlantic Council, 1975).
31. Bergsten, Fred C. and W. R. Cline, 'Conclusion and Policy Implications' in W. R. Cline (ed.), *Trade Policy in the 1980s* (Washington, DC: Institute for International Economics, 1983).
32. Hudec, R. E., *Adjudication of International Trade Disputes*, Thames Essay No. 13, London Trade Policy Research Centre, 1978.
33. Wolf, M., 'Fiddling While the GATT Burns', *The World Economy*, March 1986, pp. 1–18.

6 The Uruguay Round of Multilateral Trade Negotiations

1. *GATT Activities 1986. An Annual Review of the Work of the GATT* (Geneva: GATT, June 1987) pp. 15–29.
2. *GATT Activities in 1986. An Annual Review of the Work of the GATT* (Geneva: GATT, June 1987) pp. 16–17.
3. This is not a novel idea. Variations on this theme have been advanced by Robin Gray, in an unpublished paper for the Commonwealth Secretariat.
4. Yoffie, D. and R. O. Keohane, 'Responding to the "New Protectionism": Strategies for the ADCs' in Wontack Hong and L. B. Krause (eds), *Trade and Growth of the Advanced Developing Countries in the Pacific Basin* (Seoul: Korean Development Institute, 1981).
5. Patterson, G. and E. Patterson, 'Objectives of the Uruguay Round', in J. M. Finger and A. Olechowski, (eds), *The Uruguay Round: A Handbook*

on Multilateral Trade Negotiations (Washington, DC: The World Bank, 1987).

6. Hufbauer, G. C. and J. J. Schott, *Trading for Growth: The Next Round of Trade Negotiations* (Washington, DC: Institute for International Economics, September 1985). Refer to Chapter 2.

7. *The Uruguay Round of Multilateral Trade Negotiations* (London: Commonwealth Secretariat, November 1986) pp. 20–1.

8. Olechowski, A., 'Non-tariff Barriers to Trade' in J. M. Finger and A. Olechowski (eds), op. cit. pp. 125–6.

9. Ibid, p. 126.

10. Nam, Chong-Hyun, 'Export-Promoting Subsidies, Countervailing Threats, and the General Agreement on Tariffs and Trade', *The World Bank Economic Review*, September 1987, pp. 727–43.

11. Wolf, Alan W., 'The Need for New GATT Rules to Govern Safeguard Actions', in W. R. Cline (ed.), *Trade Policy in the 1980s* (Washington, DC: Institute for International Economics, 1985).

12. Nukazawa, K., 'Hijacking GATT While Japan Looks On', *Wall Street Journal*, 31 August, 1987.

13. Baldwin, R. E., 'GATT Reforms: Selected Issues', in H. Kierzkowski (ed.), *Protection and Competition in International Trade* (Oxford: Basil Blackwell, 1987) pp. 204–14.

14. *The Uruguay Round of Multilateral Trade Negotiations* (London: Commonwealth Secretariat, November 1986).

Bibliography

1. Agarwala, R., *Price Distortion and Growth in Developing Countries*, World Bank Staff Working Paper No. 575, (Washington, DC: World Bank, 1983).
2. Amsden, A. H., 'The Directionality of Trade: Historical Perspective and Overview' in Oli Havrylyshyn (ed.), *Exports of Developing Countries: How Directionality Affects Performance* (Washington, DC: The World Bank, 1987).
3. Anderson, K. and Y. Hayami, *The Political Economy of Agricultural Protection* (London: Allen & Unwin, 1986).
4. Anjaria, S. J. *et al*, *Trade Policy Issues and Development*, Washington DC, International Monetary Fund, Occasional Paper No. 38, July 1985.
5. The Atlantic Council, *GATT Plus: A Proposal for Trade Reform* (Washington, DC: 1975).
6. Badgett, L. D., Preferential Tariff Reduction: The Philippine Response, *Journal of International Economics*, Vol. 8, 1978 No. 1.
7. Balassa, Bela, 'Export Incentives and Export Performance in Developing Countries: A Comparative Analysis', *Weltwirtschaftliches Archiv*, Band 114 No. 1, 1978.
8. Balassa, Bela, 'Exports and Economic Growth: Further Evidence', *The Journal of Development Economies*, June 1978, pp. 181–9.
9. Balassa, Bela, 'Structural Adjustment Policy in Developing Countries', *World Development*, Vol. 10, 1982, No. 1.
10. Balassa, Bela, *Exports, Policy Choices and Economic Growth in Developing Countries After the 1973 Oil Shock*, (Washington, DC: World Bank, DRD Paper No. 48, May 1983).
11. Baldwin, R. E. and T. Murray, 'MFN Tariff Reductions and Developing Country Trade Benefits Under the GSP', *The Economic Journal*, March 1977, pp. 30–46.
12. Baldwin, R. E., 'GATT Reforms: Selected Issues', in H. Kierkowski (ed.), *Protection and Competition in International Trade* (Oxford: Basil Blackwell, 1987) pp. 204–214.
13. Bergsten, Fred C. and W. R. Cline, 'Conclusion and Policy Implications' in W. R. Cline (ed.), *Trade Policy in the 1980s* (Washington, DC: Institute for International Economies, 1983).
14. Bhagwati, J. N., 'Outward Orientation: Trade Issues' in Vittoria Corbo, M. Goldstein and M. Khan (eds), *Growth-Oriented Adjustment Programs* (Washington, DC: International Monetary Fund, 1987).
15. Bhagwati, J. N., 'Export Promoting Trade Strategy', *The World Bank Research Observer*, January 1988, pp. 27–57.
16. Bradford, Colin I., 'Rise of the NTCs as Exporters on a Global Scale', in L. Turner and N. McMuller (eds), *The Newly Industrialising Countries: Trade and Adjustment* (London: Allen & Unwin, 1982).

17. Brown, D. K., 'Trade Preferences for Developing Countries: A Survey of Results', *The Journal of Development Studies*, April 1988.
18. Cable, V., 'Textiles and Clothing' in J. M. Finger and A. Olechowski (eds), *The Uruguay Round: A Handbook on the Multilateral Trade Negotiations* (Washington, DC: The World Bank, 1987).
19. Cairncross, A., *Factors in Economic Development* (London: Allen & Unwin, 1962).
20. Cambridge Economic Policy Group, *Economic Policy Review*, (Cambridge: Cambridge University Press, 1976).
21. Chenery, H. B. and D. B. Keesing, *The Changing Composition of Developing Country Exports* (Washington, DC: World Bank Staff Working Paper, No. 314, 1979).
22. Chenery, H. B., S. Robinson and M. Syrquin, *Industrialisation and Growth: A Comparative Study* (New York: Oxford University Press, 1986).
23. Chow, P. C. Y., Causality Between Export Growth and Industrial Development', *The Journal of Development Economics*, 1987, No. 26, pp. 55–63.
24. Cizelje, B. and M. Fuks, 'Trade Among Developing Countries: Achievements and Potential' in Oli Havrylyshyn (ed.), *Exports of Developing Countries: How Direction Affects Performance* (Washington, DC: The World Bank, 1987).
25. Cline, W. R., 'Can the East Asian Model of Development Be Generalised?' *World Development*, Vol. 10, February 1982, pp. 81–90.
26. Cline, W. R., (ed.), *Trade Policies in the 1980s* (Washington, DC: Institute of International Economies, 1983).
27. Commonwealth Secretariat, *The Uruguay Round of Multilateral Trade Negotiations* (London: November 1986).
28. Cordon, Max, 'Policies Towards Market Disturbances' in H. R. Shape (ed.), *Issues in World Trade Policy* (London: Macmillan, 1986).
29. Corden, W. M., *Protection and Liberalization: A Review of Analytical Issues* (Washington, DC: International Monetary Fund, Occasional Paper No. 54, August 1987).
30. Das, Dilip K., 'Dismantling the Multifibre Arrangement?', *The Journal of World Trade Law*, January 1985, pp. 67–81.
31. Destler, I. M., *American Trade Policies: System Under Stress* (Washington, DC: Institute for International Economies, 1986).
32. Diaz-Alejandro, C. F., 'Trade Policy and Economic Development' in P. B. Kenen (ed.), *International Trade and Finance* (Cambridge: Cambridge University Press, 1975).
33. *Economist*, Economic and Financial Indicators, 3 October, 1987.
34. *Economist*, 24 October, 1987.
35. *Economist*, 'Economic and Financial Indicators', 31 October, 1987, p. 96.
36. *Economist*, 20 February, 1988.
37. Erzan, R., Samuel Laird and Alexander Yeats, *On the Potential for Expanding South-South Trade Through the Extension of Mutual Preferences Among Developing Countries* (Geneva: UNCTAD, Discussion Paper No. 16, 1986).

38. *Financial Times*, 1 March 1988.
39. Finger, J. M., 'Trade Liberalization: A Public Choice Perspective', in Ryan Amacher, G. Haberler and T. Willett (eds), *Challenge to A Liberal International Order* (Washington, DC: American Enterprise Institute, 1979).
40. The General Agreement on Tariffs and Trade, *Basic Instruments and Selected Documents* (Geneva: GATT, March 1969) Vol. IV.
41. The General Agreement on Tariffs and Trade, *Basic Instruments and Selected Documents, Twenty-Sixth Supplement* (Geneva: GATT March 1980) p. 203.
42. The General Agreement on Tariffs and Trade, *International Trade 1983/84* (Geneva: GATT 1984).
43. GATT, *Report of the Tariff Surveillance Body to the Textiles Committee*, COM/TEX/SB/984 (Geneva: GATT, October 1984).
44. GATT, *Trade Policy for a Better Future: Prospects for Action* (Geneva: GATT 1985).
45. GATT, *Developments in the Trade System. April-September 1986* (Geneva: GATT, 1987).
46. *GATT Press Communiqué*, No. 1428, 20 January 1988.
47. *GATT Press Release*, No. 1432, 29 February, 1988.
48. The General Agreement on Tariffs and Trade, *International Trade 1983–84* (Geneva: GATT, 1984).
49. The General Agreement on Tariffs and Trade, *International Trade 1985–86* (Geneva: GATT 1986).
50. The General Agreement on Tariffs and Trade, *International Trade 1986–87* (Geneva: GATT 1987).
51. The General Agreement on Tariffs and Trade, *GATT Activities 1986* (Geneva: GATT, June 1987).
52. Greenaway, D., *International Trade Policy: From Tariff to the New Protectionism* (London: Macmillan, 1983).
53. Greenaway, D. and C. H. Nam, 'Industrialisation and Macroeconomic Performance in Developing Countries Under Alternative Trade Strategies', *Kyklos*, Vol. 41, Fasc. 3, 1988.
54. Haberler, G., 'Liberal and Illiberal Development Policy', in G. M. Meir (ed.), *Pioneers in Development* (New York: Oxford University Press, Second Series, 1987).
55. Havrylyshyn, O., *Penetrating the Fallacy of Export Composition or Honbson's Second Falsehood Revisited* (Washington, DC: World Bank, November 1986) mimeo.
56. Havrylyshyn, O. and I. Alikhani, 'Is there cause for Export Optimism? An Enquiry into the Evidence of a Second-Generation of Successful Exports', *Weltwirtschaftliches Archiv*, Vol. 118, 1982, pp. 651–62.
57. Havrylyshyn, O. and M. Wolf, *Trade Among Developing Countries: Theory, Policy Issues and Principal Trends* (Washington, DC: World Bank Staff Working Paper No. 479, 1981).
58. Hudec, R. E., *Adjudication of International Trade Disputes* Thames Essay No. 13, (London: Trade Policy Research Centre, 1978).
59. Haufbauer, G. C. and J. J. Schoot, *Trading for Growth: The Next Round of Trade Negotiations* (Washington, DC: Institute for Interna-

tional Economies, September 1985).

60. Hughes, H. and J. Wallbrocke, 'Can Developing Country Exports Keep Growing in the 1980s?' *The World Economy*, June 1981, pp. 127–47.

61. International Monetary Fund, *Direction of Trade Statistics 1987* (Washington, DC: IMF, 1987).

62. Jung-ho, Yoo, *Free Trade Without Fair Trade is Unsustainable* (Seoul, Korea: Korean Development Institute, 1985).

63. Karsenty, G. and S. Laird, *The Generalised System of Preferences: A Quantitative Assessment of the Direct Trade Effects and of Policy Options* (Geneva: UNCTAD, Discussion Paper No. 18, 1986).

64. Kim, K. S., 'Lessons from South Korea's Experience with Industrialisation, in Vithorio Carbo, *et al.* (eds), *Export-Oriented Development Strategies* (Boulder: Westview Press, 1985).

65. Kestecki, M., 'Export-restraint Arrangements and Trade Liberalization', *The World Economy*, December 1987.

66. Krueger, A. O., 'Export Prospects and Economic Growth: India: A Comment', *The Economic Journal*, June 1961, pp. 436–42.

67. Krueger, A. O., *Foreign Trade Regimes and Economic Development: Liberalisation Attempts and Consequences* (New York: Columbia University Press for NBER, 1978).

68. Krueger, Anne O. and C. Michalopoulos, 'Developing Country, Trade Policies, and International Economic Systems' in E. H. Preeg (ed.), *Hard Bargaining Ahead: US Trade Policy and Developing Countries* (New Brunswick: Transaction Books, 1985).

69. Krueger, Anne O., 'The Experience and Lessons of Asia's Super Exporters', in Vittorio Corbo, *et al.* (eds), *Export Oriented Development Strategies* (Boulder: Westview Press, 1985) pp. 187–248.

70. Lal, D., *The Poverty of Development Economies* (London: Institute of Economic Affairs, 1984).

71. Lal, D. and S. Rajapatirana, 'Foreign Trade Regimes and Economic Growth in Developing Countries', *Research Observer*, July 1987.

72. Lall, S., 'South-South Economic Co-operation and Global Negotiations', J. N. Bhagawati and J. G. Ruggie (eds), *Power Passions and Purpose* (Cambridge, Mass.: MIT Press, 1984).

73. Lande, S. and C. Vangrasstek, *Trade and Tariff Act of 1984* (Massachusetts: Lexington, 1986).

74. Larson, E. D., M. H. Ross and R. H. Williams, 'Beyond the Era of Materials', *Scientific American*, Vol. 254, June 1986, No. 6.

75. Lewis, W. A., 'The Slowing Down of the Engine of Growth', *The American Economic Review*, September 1980, pp. 555–64.

76. Little, I. M. D., *Economic Development, Theory Policy and International Relations* (New York: Basic Books, 1982).

77. Little, I. M. D., T. Scitovsky and M. Scott, *Industry and Trade in some Developing Countries: A Comparative Study* (London: Oxford University Press, 1970).

78. Lorenz, D., 'New Situations Facing the NICs in East Asia', *Intereconomies*, November/December 1986, pp. 263–368.

79. Maizels, A., *Industrial Growth and World Trade* (Cambridge: Cambridge University Press, 1963).

80. Michalopoulos, C. and Keith Jay, *Growth of Exports and Income in the Developing World: A Neoclassical View*, AID Discussion Paper No. 28 (Washington, DC: Agency for International Development, 1973).
81. Michaley, M., 'Exports and Growth: An Empirical Investigation', *The Journal of Development Economies*, March 1977, pp. 49–53.
82. Murray, T., *Trade Preferences for Developing Countries* (London: Macmillan, 1977).
83. Nam, Choythyum, 'Export-Promoting Subsidies, Countervailing Threats, and the General Agreement on Tariffs and Trade', *The World Bank Economic Review*, September 1987, pp. 727–43.
84. Nukazawa, K., 'Hijacking GATT While Japan Looks on', *The Wall Street Journal*, 31 August, 1987.
85. Nurkse, R., *Equilibrium and Growth in the World Economy* (Cambridge, Mass.: Harvard University Press, 1961).
86. Nusbaumer, J., *The Service Economy: Lever to Growth* (Boston: Kluwer Academic Publications, 1987).
87. Organisation for Economic Co-operation and Development, *The Impact of Newly Industrialising Countries on Production and Trade in Manufactures* (Paris: OECD, 1979).
88. Organisation of Economic Co-operation and Development, *The Generalised System of Preferences, Review of the First Decade* (Paris: OECD, 1983).
89. Organisation of Economic Co-operation and Development, *Costs and Benefits of Protectionism* (Paris: OECD, 1985).
90. Organisation of Economic Co-operation and Development, *Economic Relations Between Developed and Developing Countries: Situation and Prospects* (Paris: OECD, 1986).
91. Patterson, G. and E. Patterson, 'Objectives of the Uruguay Round' in J. M. Finger and A. Olechowski (eds), *The Uruguay Round: A Handbook on Multilateral Trade Negotiations* (Washington, DC: The World Bank, 1987).
92. Pelzman, J. and G. K. Schaepfle, 'The Impact of the Caribbean Basin Economic Recovery Act on Caribbean Nation's Exports and Development', mimeo, 1986.
93. Ranis, G., 'Challenge and Opportunities Posed by Asia's Superexporters' in W. Baer and M. Gillis (eds), *Export Diversification and the New Protectionism* (Urbana: University of Illinois, 1981).
94. Ranis, G., 'Can the East Asian Model of Development Be Generalised? A Comment', *World Development*, Vol. 13, 1985, No. 4, pp. 543–45.
95. Rhee, Y. W., *Instruments for Export Policy and Administration*, World Bank Staff Working Paper, No. 725 (Washington, DC: World Bank, March 1985).
96. Riddle, D., *Service-led Growth* (New York: Praeger, 1986).
97. Riedel, J., *Myths and Reality of External Constraints on Development* (London: Gover for Trade Policy Research Centre, 1987).
98. Rousslong, D. and J. Lindsey, 'The Benefit of Caribbean Basin Countries from the US CBI Tariff Elimination', *Journal of Policy Modelling*, Vol. 6, 1984, No. 4.

99. Sampson, G. P. and R. H. Snape, 'Identifying the Issues in Trade in Services, *The World Economy*, 1985, No. 8, pp. 171–81.
100. Sapir, A., North-South Issues in Trade in Services, *The World Economy*, March 1985, pp. 27–41.
101. Sapir, A. and L. Lundberg, 'The U.S. Generalised System of preferences and Its Impact' in Robert E. Baldwin and Anne O. Krueger, (eds), *American Trade Relations*, II (Chicago: University of Chicago Press, 1986).
102. Sawyer, W. C. and R. L. Sprinkle, 'Caribbean Basin Economic Recovery Act: Export Expansion Effects', *Journal of World Trade Law*, Vol. 18, 1984, No. 5.
103. Schumacher, D., 'Imports from Developing Countries: Reasons for Protection and Proposal for Liberalization', *Intereconomics*, November/December 1984.
104. Selowsky, M., 'Adjustment in the 1980s: An Overview of Issues', *Finance and Development*, June 1987.
105. Streeten, P., A Cool look at Outward-Looking Strategies for Development', *World Economy*, September 1982, pp. 159–69.
106. Tsiang, S. C., 'Foreign Trade and Investment As Booster for Take-off: The Experience of Taiwan', In Vittorio Carbo, *et al* (ed.), *Export Oriented Development Strategies* (Boulder: Westview Press, 1985).
107. Tymowski, M. J., 'Trade Information System on Barriers to Trade Among Developing Countries' in Oli Havrylyshyn (ed.), *Exports of Developing Countries: How Direction Affects Performance* (Washington, DC: The World Bank, 1987).
108. Tumlir, J., 'Emergency Protection Against Sharp Increases in Imports' in H. Corbet and R. Vackson (eds), *Effective Tariff Protection* (London: Croom Helm, 1971).
109. UNCTAD, *Protection, Trade Restrictions and Structural Adjustment* (Geneva: UNCTAD, June 1983) pp. 11–14.
110. UNCTAD, *Ministerial Declaration on the Global System at Trade Preferences among Developing Countries (GSTP/L, 24)* (New Delhi: UNCTAD, July 1985).
111. UNCTAD, '*Impact of New and Emerging Technologies on Trade and Development*', TD/B/C/.6/136, August 1986.
112. UNCTAD, *Revitalizing Development, Growth and International Trade* (Geneva: UNCTAD, July 1987).
113. UNCTAD, *Statistical Note by the UNCTAD Secretariat*, TD/B/C.7/86 (Geneva: UNCTAD, 16 June 1988).
114. UNIDO, *World Industry Since 1960s: Progress and Prospects* (New York: United Nations, 1979).
115. The U.S. Congress, Sub-committee on International Trade, *Generalised System of Preferences* (Washington, DC: 1986).
116. Valdes, A., 'Agriculture in Uruguay Round: Interest of "Developing Countries"', *The World Bank Economic Review*, September 1987.
117. Whally, J., *Trade Liberalisation Among Major World Trading Area* (Cambridge, Mass.: MIT Press, 1985).
118. Wolf, Alan W., 'The Need for New GATT Rules to Govern Safeguard Actions', in W. R. Cline (ed.), *Trade Policy in 1980s* (Washington, DC:

Institute for International Economies, 1985).

119. Wolf, M., 'Fiddling While the GATT Burns', *The World Economy*, March 1986, pp. 1–18.

120. World Bank, *Linkage Between Trade and Promotion of Development* (Washington, DC: World Bank, 1986) pp. 29–30.

121. World Bank, *World Development Report, 1987* (Washington, DC: Oxford University Press, June 1987).

122. Yeats, A. J., 'A Comparative Analysis of Tariffs and Transport Costs on India's Exports', *The Journal of Development Studies*, 1977, No. 1, pp. 97–107.

123. Yeats, A. J., *Trade and Development Policy: Leading Issues for the 1980s* (London: Macmillan, 1983).

124. Yoffie, D., and R. O. Keohome, 'Responding to the "New Protectionism": Strategies for the ADC' in Wontack Hong and L. B. Krause (eds), *Trade and Growth of the Advance Developing Countries in the Pacific Basin* (Seoul: Korean Development Institute, 1981).

Index